Human Aspects of Air Force Operations

The Roles of Social, Cultural,
and Political Knowledge and Skills
in the Full Spectrum of Multidomain Operations

KIRSTEN M. KELLER, DAVID E. THALER, KATHLEEN REEDY,
CAROLINE BAXTER, RYAN HABERMAN, WILLIAM MACKENZIE,
MIRIAM MATTHEWS, PHILLIP PADILLA, YULIYA SHOKH

Prepared for the United States Air Force
Approved for public release; distribution unlimited

RAND PROJECT AIR FORCE

For more information on this publication, visit www.rand.org/t/RR3221

Library of Congress Cataloging-in-Publication Data is available for this publication.
ISBN: 978-1-9774-0548-7

Published by the RAND Corporation, Santa Monica, Calif.
© Copyright 2020 RAND Corporation
RAND® is a registered trademark.

Cover image: DVIDS/Staff Sgt. Patrick Evenson

Support RAND
Make a tax-deductible charitable contribution at
www.rand.org/giving/contribute

www.rand.org

Preface

Countering emerging threats is not based solely on defeating a nation-state's military forces by conventional, kinetic means. Fundamentally, these threats are met by understanding and manipulating the human aspects that drive the adversary's ideological narrative within the target population and are an important consideration in influencing their actions. For example, as Russian manipulation of American social media and Chinese use of information warfare demonstrate, understanding how local populations and foreign governments will read and react to different stimuli is essential to operating in the competition space. These types of threats demand that the U.S. military understand the human aspects of military operations, or the social, cultural, physical, informational, and psychological elements that determine our partner nations' and adversaries' motivations, thinking, influence, activities, and recruitment.

This report explores whether there is a need for a joint warfighting domain focused on human aspects of military operations and considers how sociocultural knowledge and skills related to human aspects of war could be better integrated into conventional Air Force multi-domain operations. The research reported here was commissioned by Air Force Special Operations Command and conducted within the Manpower, Personnel, and Training Program of RAND Project AIR FORCE as part of a fiscal year 2018 project, "Integrating the Human Domain into Air Force Multi-Domain Operations."

RAND Project AIR FORCE

RAND Project AIR FORCE (PAF), a division of the RAND Corporation, is the Department of the Air Force's (DAF's) federally funded research and development center for studies and analyses. PAF provides the DAF with independent analyses of policy alternatives affecting the development, employment, combat readiness, and support of current and future air, space, and cyber forces. Research is conducted in four programs: Strategy and Doctrine; Force Modernization and Employment; Manpower, Personnel, and Training; and Resource Management. The research reported here was prepared under contract FA7014-16-D-1000.

Additional information about PAF is available on our website:
www.rand.org/paf/.

This report documents work originally shared with the Department of the Air Force in September 2018. The draft report, issued on September 27, 2018, was reviewed by formal peer reviewers and DAF subject-matter experts.

Contents

Tables

Summary

The 2018 *National Defense Strategy* (NDS) emphasizes the threat to U.S. interests posed by "the reemergence of long-term strategic competition, rapid dispersion of technologies, and new concepts of warfare and competition that span the entire spectrum of conflict" (Department of Defense [DoD], 2018). As revisionist, near-peer powers, China and Russia are noted as the most important competitors, both in terms of influence and capability, while Iran and North Korea remain formidable "rogue" regimes, and violent extremist groups like ISIL and al Qaeda continue to threaten terror attacks. In answering the strategy's call for a "more lethal, resilient, and rapidly innovating Joint Force," the U.S. Air Force and the other services are placing considerable emphasis on integrating the broad range of U.S. operational capabilities into multi-domain operations as a means of addressing complex threats. While the concept involves harnessing new, more lethal technologies and concepts of operation, it also recognizes that war has never been primarily about destruction. It has always been a contest of opposing independent wills, and force has always been a tool used to manipulate an adversary's will to fight. Multi-domain operations are ultimately aimed at influencing adversaries and operating with allies. To do both of these with the greatest efficiency, the Air Force must understand where the best leverage points are and how to best utilize them with the application of air, space, and cyber power. An understanding of human aspects of military operations—or the social, cultural, political, and psychological elements that determine the motivations and actions of both our partner nations and our adversaries—plays a role in identifying these leverage points.

Recognizing this imperative in warfare, the Joint Staff in 2016 published the *Joint Concept for Human Aspects of Military Operations* (JC-HAMO), a concept of operations that offers a framework to enable the military services to incorporate human-focused capabilities into their training, planning, and organizational culture. However, whereas the special operations community and other services have focused on leveraging human-focused capabilities, the conventional Air Force has yet to fully embrace human aspects of military operations. Whether in "traditional" or "irregular" warfare, the NDS charges the Joint Force, including the Air Force, with finding ways to "enhance operations by impacting the will and influencing the decisionmaking of relevant actors in the environment, shaping their behavior, both active and passive, in a manner that is consistent with U.S. objectives" (JC-HAMO, 2016, p. 1).

Human aspects of war are essential to Air Force success in all prospective operations. Improving understanding of the human aspects can help it contribute directly to joint activities like influence operations and advising, but also high-order warfighting. If air commanders understand U.S. adversaries, then they can better direct strike missions to influence their will to fight. If they better understand U.S. allies, they will be able to better assess the likelihood that they will provide support when needed in a major war. And, if the U.S. Air Force (USAF) can apply this thinking to adversaries and allies, then it can better apply it to its own institutional needs.

Motivated by the growing relevance of the human aspects of military operations, Air Force Special Operations Command asked RAND Project AIR FORCE (PAF) to conduct a study to determine whether there is a need for a new warfighting domain—the "human domain"—and to explore how sociocultural knowledge and capabilities related to this concept could be better integrated into *conventional* Air Force multi-domain operations, an emerging concept that is aimed at systematically integrating capabilities in two or more warfighting domains (air, land, sea, space, cyberspace) to attain significant strategic, operational, and tactical effects.

To address these issues, the RAND PAF team reviewed USAF and military doctrine, concepts, and policies relating to human aspects of military operations, as well as reviewed relevant military and academic literature. The research team then conducted interviews with over 200 subject-matter experts (SMEs) and key stakeholders within the Air Force, the broader U.S. military, and two select international partner militaries (the UK and Germany) to better understand what and how human-domain-related efforts might currently be incorporated into training, skill sets, and planning and operations. Based on the literature review and insights from the SME interviews, we developed recommendations for how to better incorporate human-aspects considerations into current Air Force multi-domain operations. We summarize our key findings and recommendations below.

Is There a Need for a Human Domain?

The idea of developing a formal joint warfighting domain for human aspects of military operations is not new. Despite much debate in the past, however, efforts focused on establishing a new warfighting domain in this area never gained traction, and the need for cultural competence and knowledge became associated primarily with irregular warfare. As a key component of this study, we again explored the idea of a human domain and uncovered many of the same arguments that served as barriers in the past. For example, although there appears to be general agreement that it is important to emphasize and ensure that the U.S. military develop human-focused capabilities, we found hesitation about the theoretical need for a distinct human domain and concerns regarding the pragmatic constraints on resources that would make developing a new domain challenging. Instead, stakeholders argued that it is more important for each service to recognize its own need for such capabilities and develop them, even if done so in concert with each other. Overall, interviewees felt that if the military is not taking into consideration sociocultural understandings and how to influence people, then it has lost sight of the fact that warfare is intrinsically a human endeavor, and it will never be a truly effective force.

Therefore, based on the study findings, we conclude that instead of creating a separate human domain, the services and the Joint Force should focus efforts on better integrating human aspects of military operations. There is a strong need for the services, including the Air Force, to develop and maintain human-domain-type capabilities. Moreover, with the development and publication of the JC-HAMO, the Air Force has an opportunity to further articulate the human-aspects needs of the Air Force, develop them into Air Force doctrine, and determine where and how to spend resources on developing the needed capabilities. The remainder of this study focuses on assessing those Air Force needs and where there may be gaps in current capabilities and utilization.

How Can the Air Force Improve Integration of Human Aspects into Multi-Domain Operations?

As a first step in our study, we assessed the degree to which human aspects are recognized in five relevant mission areas: strategic and operational planning, intelligence, security cooperation (SC), cyberspace, and space. We also reviewed a few smaller mission areas that require such consideration. Although we found evidence that human aspects of military operations were considered to some degree in Air Force doctrine and activities, we found that the concept is not systematically institutionalized in the conventional Air Force, and that existing capabilities related to human aspects of military operations failed to meet needed capabilities in several mission areas. Based on our review of current training and education in the Air Force, we found that although there is some acknowledgment of the importance of human-aspects-related knowledge and skills in certain places, there is no unifying terminology, and there is a lack of coordination or systematization of education and training. At the operational level, we also found gaps in available education and training in relevant career fields (e.g., intelligence, cyber, and space) to meet the needs for human-aspects-related capabilities.

Developing and integrating these capabilities should not be and does not have to be at the expense of developing airpower, cyber, and space expertise. Further, not all airmen need to be experts in understanding the human aspects of military operations, but developing this knowledge and these skill sets in a more planned and coordinated effort throughout the Air Force will provide the greatest benefit for operations. We also identified frameworks for integrating human aspects from other service partners and foreign military partners that the Air Force can potentially adopt in these efforts.

Recommendations

Institutional Recommendations

There is a need in the Air Force for baseline, across-the-board understanding and integration of human aspects of military operations as well as more focused education and training efforts in particular specializations. Based on the study findings, we identified several institutional-level recommendations that we believe are critical to begin to more effectively integrate human-aspects considerations into multi-domain operations.

- ***Develop USAF guidance that reflects the JC-HAMO:*** Human aspects are an essential part of modern Air Force operations from the strategic to the tactical level and will be a vital set of capabilities going forward. We therefore recommend that the Air Force leverage the JC-HAMO to develop the Air Force's own internal guidance about who should be knowledgeable in human aspects of military operations and how that information should be used to ensure it is consistently and systematically applied.

- *Better integrate human aspects into Air Force strategic planning and operations.* This includes highlighting human aspects of military operations in senior-leader communications to ensure that Air Force culture values not only high technology but also the effects that the application of airpower can have on target populations. In addition, better incorporate consideration of human aspects into wargames and exercises.
- *Cultivate SC skills within the Air Force.* Air Force senior leaders must communicate the importance of engaging in SC that relates directly to human aspects of military operations and ensure that SC positions are viewed as a positive mark on an airman's record during promotion considerations.
- *Develop mission assessment plans that provide insight into the effects of the human aspects of military operations.* Because the human environment does not always lend itself to quantifiable measures of effectiveness, we recommend exploring ways to incorporate qualitative and longitudinal evaluation means into assessments of target audiences and mission success.

Training and Education Recommendations

A key component of institutionalizing the importance of human-aspects considerations in multi-domain operations is ensuring that airmen are provided exposure to these concepts early on and that it is then reinforced or expanded upon as needed as they progress in their careers. Based on these study findings, we identified several training- and education-related recommendations for helping improve knowledge and skills related to human aspects in military operations.

- *Give airmen (officers and enlisted) an introduction to human aspects in military operations early in their careers.* Within basic military training for enlisted airmen and through the various officer-commissioning sources, ensure that requirements include exposure to the social sciences and the role of human aspects in military operations. This could provide a foundation for further professional military education.
- *Institutionalize required human-aspects curricula at all levels of air education and training.* Human aspects of military operations need to be part of the required curriculum of education and training programs across the Air Force. Such education is critical for developing planners and senior leaders who consider and value sociocultural knowledge and capabilities. This does not mean that every airman needs to be an expert in the topic, but that every airman at least be exposed to these concepts. Experts can and should be leveraged as needed.
- *Identify a centralized institution to take responsibility for human-aspects education coordination.* Curricula on human aspects are most effective if they build on previous education and training. Ensuring that there is one centralized office responsible for coordinating this courseware will help to ensure consistency and reduce ad hoc training. The Air Force Cultural and Language Center (AFCLC) or perhaps the information operations (IO) technical training schoolhouse are two potential options.
- *Better incorporate nonkinetic effects into education for planners.* Air planners have a tendency to focus on kinetic effects as the primary solution for many military problem

sets. Nonkinetic effects working instead of or, more likely, in tandem with kinetic effects will likely produce the most effective, efficient outcomes and will help mature the planning process.

- ***Institutionalize cross-cultural skills training for a wider variety of personnel.*** Tactical cross-cultural skills training currently provided to air advisors would be beneficial to many more Air Force personnel. All deploying forces, overseas base commanders, people involved in overseas acquisitions, security forces, hospitality, and instructors could benefit from having access to these courses and attaining these critical skills.

Recommendations for Developing Regional Human-Aspects Expertise

As a final component to improving the integration of human-aspects considerations into multi-domain operations, our study findings also point to several areas in which more specific regional human-aspects expertise could be further developed and utilized. In particular, we recommend that the Air Force better resource and utilize Air Force–specific reachback capabilities and have identified several options for helping further develop the required regional human-aspects expertise.

- ***Consider developing a special experience identifier for regional expertise at the enlisted level.*** Having enlisted airmen identified as having relevant regional experience may allow for the development of regional expertise that could then be leveraged for use in multiple mission areas.
- ***Consider aligning IO officers and enlisted personnel by geographic region.*** Coding and regionally aligning information operations (IO) personnel, similar to how Army Civil Affairs and Psychological Operations personnel have been used in the past, could allow them to develop methodological and regional expertise and be used more effectively in mission planning and execution.
- ***Consider developing a specialized reservist capability.*** The British construct of specialized reservists who are selectively recruited based on specific thematic or regional expertise and who would be assigned to a single unit and could support a wide range of missions as a reachback capability during their time on duty is one possible model. Using reservists rather than civilians or contractors brings military perspective into the relevant processes and allows them to be deployable if needed.

Human aspects are an inherent element of warfare. Understanding how and where to best influence target audiences can serve as a force multiplier across a wide range of operations. By incorporating the JC-HAMO into Air Force doctrine and developing the capability and understanding to operate in the human-aspects context at the strategic to tactical level, the Air Force can begin to pave the way to an ever more effective force.

Acknowledgments

We are grateful to many people who were involved in this research. In particular, we would like to thank our Air Force research sponsors, Brig Gen Sean Farrell and Brig Gen David Harris (respectively, former and current directors, Strategic Plans, Programs and Requirements, Air Force Special Operations Command), and action officer Aryea Gottlieb for their strategic guidance and perspectives throughout this study, as well as Bruce Duncan, Billy Montgomery, Daniel Snyder, Craig Werenskjold, and Lt Col Scott Scheno, who all provided a wealth of support and insight. Ray Conley, Director of Project AIR FORCE's Manpower, Personnel, and Training Program, provided much-appreciated oversight and encouragement.

We are also grateful to all the individuals we spoke with across the United States Air Force, the sister services, and international partners for their insight and input into this study. These institutions include: Air Force Special Operations Command, 6th Special Operations Squadron, U.S. Air Force Special Operations School, Headquarters Air Force A2, Air Forces International Affairs (SAF/IA), Air Education and Training Command, Basic Military Training, numerous technical training schoolhouses, Profession of Arms Center of Excellence, the Air Force Culture and Language Center, LeMay Center, Air University, the Air Advisor Flight, 818th and 571st Mobility Support and Advisory Squadrons, National Air and Space Intelligence Center, 17th Intelligence Squadron, 67th Cyberspace Wing, United States Air Forces Europe and Air Forces Africa, the Inter-European Air Force Academy, the United States Air Forces Europe Band, Special Operations Command, Joint Information Operations Warfare Center, United States Army Special Operations Command, United States Army John F. Kennedy Special Warfare Center and School, the Training Support Center Quantico, the German Center for Cross-Cultural Communications, the German Air Force Officer School, the British Defence Cultural Specialist Unit, the British 77th Group, the Defence Geographic Centre, the Defence and Science Technology Laboratory, Defence Intelligence community, and the Johns Hopkins University Applied Physics Lab. We also thank individual contributors from Office of Special Investigations, Cyber, Space, Intelligence, Information Operations, Psychological Operations, Civil Affairs, and numerous other career fields for providing invaluable information on their experiences and understanding of human aspects of military operations.

We thank our technical reviewers, Jeannie Johnson, Director of the Center for Anticipatory Intelligence at Utah State University, and RAND colleagues Beth Grill and Ben Connable for their insightful feedback and comments on the draft of this report. Their reviews significantly strengthened its final quality.

Finally, this research would not have been possible without the support of a wide range of other RAND colleagues, including administrative support inexhaustibly provided by Cecile St. Julien, Julie Ann Tajiri, and Christina Dozier. And, as ever, we are indebted to Barbara Bicksler for taking a string of words and shaping it into a report.

Abbreviations

AETC	Air Education and Training Command
AFAFRICA	Air Force Africa
AFCLC	Air Force Culture and Language Center
AFDD	Air Force Doctrine Document
AFECD	*Air Force Enlisted Classification Directory*
AFMC	Air Force Materiel Command
AFRL	Air Force Research Laboratory
AFSC	Air Force specialty code
AFSOC	Air Force Special Operations Command
ARSOF	Army Special Operations Forces
BMT	basic military training
CAA	Combat Aviation Advisor
CAOCL	Center for Advanced Operational Culture Learning
COA	course of action
DCSU	Defence Cultural Specialist Unit
DoD	Department of Defense
DoDD	Department of Defense Directive
DoDI	Department of Defense Instruction
FAO	Foreign Area Officer
HAF	Headquarters Air Force
HUMINT	human intelligence
IEAFA	Inter-European Air Forces Academy
IO	information operations
IPOE	intelligence preparation of the operational environment
ISR	intelligence, surveillance, and reconnaissance

JC-HAMO	*Joint Concept for Human Aspects of Military Operations*
JIOWC	Joint Information Operations Warfare Center
JP	Joint Publication
JSOU	Joint Special Operations University
LEAP	Language Enabled Airmen Program
LREC	language, regional expertise, and culture
M&S	modeling and simulation
MCDP	Marine Corps Doctrinal Publication
MCIA	Marine Corps Intelligence Activity
MCO	Marine Corps Order
MIG	Marine Expeditionary Information Group
MISO	Military Information Support Operations
MOS	military occupational specialty
MSAS	Mobility Support and Advisory Squadron
NASIC	National Air and Space Intelligence Center
NATO	North Atlantic Treaty Organization
NCOA	noncommissioned officer academy
OSI	Office of Special Investigations
PACE	Professional Arms Center of Excellence
PME	professional military education
RCLF	regional, culture, and language familiarization
SASO	Stability Operations
SC	security cooperation
SFAB	Security Forces Assistance Brigade
SME	subject-matter expert
SOF	Special Operations Forces
SOS	Squadron Officer School
TRADOC	Training and Doctrine Command

UCMJ	Uniform Code of Military Justice
USAF	U.S. Air Force
USAFA	U.S. Air Force Academy
USAFE	U.S. Air Forces in Europe
USASOC	U.S. Army Special Operations Command
USSOCOM	U.S. Special Operations Command

1. Introduction

That war is a human endeavor rooted in a social context has been a well-understood theory for millennia, dating back to Sun Tzu's *The Art of War* and Carl von Clausewitz's treatise *On War*. The definitive Byzantine manual on war, the *Strategikon*, devoted an entire chapter to understanding different populations and how cultural values and preferences influence operational behavior during conflict. For example, it noted that the Slavs and Antes "have many kings among them always at odds with one another, [so] it is not difficult to win over some of them . . . and then to attack the others, so that their common hostility will not make them united or bring them together under one ruler," while Franks and Lombards are "easily corrupted by money, greedy as they are," and "although they possess bold and daring spirits, their bodies are pampered and soft . . . they are hurt by heat, cold, rain, [and] lack of provisions, especially of wine" (Maurice, 1984, pp. 123, 119). More recent, twentieth-century experiences point to the centrality of human elements of warfare—and the effects of a failure to properly analyze them—as a fundamental component of outcomes on the battlefield. In the Battle of Verdun during World War I, inaccurate German association of the low morale and exhaustion of French prisoners of war with the morale, cohesion, and readiness of the French defensive lines led to failure to achieve German objectives, at the cost of 300,000 lives on each side (Connable, 2018, pp. 15–17). And in 1967, a year before North Vietnam's massive Tet Offensive that ultimately led to the U.S. withdrawal from Vietnam and consolidation of communist power, U.S. leaders were assessing that North Vietnamese forces were at a "crossover point" and close to breaking, while North Vietnam's leader, Ho Chi Minh, was declaring that "you can kill ten of my men for every one I kill of yours, but even at those odds, you will lose and I will win" (as quoted in Karnow, 1998).[1]

Evidence of integrating the human element in military operations is not limited to bygone eras. Clausewitz is quoted extensively in U.S. joint doctrine (Joint Publication [JP] 1, 2017), and Clausewitzian conceptions of warfare lie at the heart of joint military education, training, and, ostensibly, operations. Understanding the human element is not a "nice-to-have"—it is supposed to be the way the entire Joint Force conceptualizes war. And the human element is deeply embedded in the doctrine of U.S. adversaries. The book *Unrestricted Warfare*, ostensibly written by two Chinese Air Force colonels,[2] states that "the new principles of war . . . no longer use armed forces to compel the enemy to submit to one's will, but instead use all means, including armed force or non-armed force, military and non-military, and lethal and non-lethal means to

---

[1] Ho Chi Minh made this declaration in the context of his understanding that human beings and their will to fight are more important than superior weapons and firepower.

[2] There is some question as to the document's authenticity, but its concepts are debated in Western defense communities. See Connable, Campbell, and Madden, 2016, p. 3.

compel the enemy to accept one's interests" (Lee, 2014, p. 201). This quote is a cornerstone of modern Chinese military doctrine and stems from a long history of including "political work" as a part of military operations, recognizing the importance of human-focused capabilities in winning wars.

From this starting point, the People's Liberation Army developed the "Three Warfares" doctrine, which emphasizes the importance of psychological operations, public opinion warfare, and legal warfare as military capabilities (Lee, 2014). This approach focuses on influencing the decisions of outside players (and internal ones as well) through various means of messaging aimed at specific audiences (e.g., insisting that China has no interest in hegemony), influencing regional partners (e.g., messaging to U.S. allies in Southeast Asia to drive wedges between them and the United States), and the manipulation of legal boundaries (e.g., the various disputed territories) (Coyer, 2015). China very much sees this type of information or political warfare as a military function and, in doing so, relies heavily on knowledge and understanding of the social, cultural, and political dynamics of the target audiences.

Russia has also demonstrated an ability to operate effectively in the information and human environments. For example, in conjunction with military activities, Moscow used "economic coercion and information operations to destabilize Ukraine's government" and meddled in their elections (Grady, 2017). These actions, in addition to the attempted manipulation of American sentiments through the use of social media bots (Westervelt, 2017) are all indications that Russia is fully capable of operationalizing social, cultural, and political knowledge for military and political purposes. Knowing what works on which populations and why, or at least learning by investing in strong preparatory measures, is key to such efforts.

The Human Element in U.S. Military Concepts of Operation

In the U.S. military, understanding of the social, cultural, and political dynamics of the target audiences is commonly perceived to be most relevant in irregular warfare or insurgency situations, where forces are focused on understanding and addressing the grievances of the local population to ensure that they do not support insurgents. However, the strategic emphasis at the national level has largely shifted away from counterinsurgency missions to focus on the competitive environment with peer and near-peer countries (DoD, 2018). Consideration of human aspects of military operations do not become less important in such scenarios, however. As Russian manipulation of American social media and Chinese use of information warfare demonstrate, understanding how local populations and foreign governments will read and react to different stimuli is essential to operating in the competition space and will be as or more relevant in the case of more traditional, high-end warfare given the modern world's reliance on the information environment.

The joint community has recognized the importance of human aspects in military operations across the spectrum of conflict and as a key element of "multi-domain operations." The concept of multi-domain operations generally refers to the systematic integration of capabilities across two or more warfighting domains (air, land, sea, space, and cyberspace) to achieve offensive and defensive military effects from the strategic to the tactical levels. However, there is no widely accepted definition, nor is there common understanding of what a concept of operations entails (see Spirtas, 2018).

In October 2016, the Joint Staff published the *Joint Concept for Human Aspects of Military Operations* (JC-HAMO), a concept of operations that offers a framework to enable the military services to incorporate human-focused capabilities into their training, planning, and organizational culture. The JC-HAMO notes that

> human aspects are the interactions among humans and between humans and the environment that influence decisions. . . . To be effective at these interactions, the Joint Force must analyze and understand the social, cultural, physical, informational, and psychological elements that influence behavior. (JC-HAMO, 2016, p. 1)

The concept emphasizes that "all echelons of our force must have a foundational understanding of what drives human behavior" (JC-HAMO, 2016, p. i). In our treatment of human aspects of military operations, we employ the term "human-focused capabilities" to reflect incorporation of the understanding, training, and operational exploitation of human aspects into the skill sets of military personnel based on the requirements of their career fields or positions. For example, a commander who directs a conventional campaign against an adversary should base his decisions in part on a deep appreciation of the will and influence of key actors on the battlefield; he would be considered as possessing human-focused capability. Human-focused capabilities have long played a central role in the U.S. special operations community and, with their institutionalization through the JC-HAMO, in the joint community and some of the military services.

However, as discussed in this report, the conventional Air Force has yet to fully embrace human aspects of military operations. These human-focused capabilities will play an important role in a world that is increasingly connected. An important consideration in influencing adversary actions will come from countering the human aspects that drive an adversary's ideological goals— which requires an understanding of the social, cultural, physical, informational, and psychological elements that determine the motivations and actions of both our partner nations and our adversaries. Whether in "traditional" or "irregular" warfare, the Joint Force, including the Air Force, must find ways to "enhance operations by impacting the will and influencing the decisionmaking of relevant actors in the environment, shaping their behavior, both active and passive, in a manner that is consistent with U.S. objectives" (JC-HAMO, 2016, p. 1).

Study Objective and Approach

Motivated by the growing relevance of human aspects of military operations, in fiscal year 2018 Air Force Special Operations Command (AFSOC) asked RAND Project AIR FORCE to conduct a study to determine whether there is a need for a new warfighting domain—the human domain—and to explore how sociocultural knowledge and capabilities related to this concept could systematically be integrated into *conventional* Air Force multi-domain operations.

The study sought to answer the following key research questions:

- Is there a precedent and need for a human domain or alternative form of doctrine for conventional Air Force operations?
- What is the current state of human-focused efforts and related doctrine within the Air Force?
- Are there similar concepts or existing models for human-focused efforts in the broader U.S. military and international partners that would be relevant for the Air Force?
- What are training and education needs in the Air Force related to human-focused capabilities?

We took a multimethod approach to answer each of the above research questions. First, we reviewed relevant published concepts, policy, and doctrine. This included not only the 2016 JC-HAMO itself, but also DoD directives, publications by the Joint Chiefs of Staff, and U.S. and allied service doctrinal publications (a full list can be found in Appendix A). We also reviewed other relevant literature in academia and the military discussing human-domain-related concepts. Among the sources were RAND reports, articles from U.S. military educational institutions, and peer-reviewed journal articles on human and other warfighting domains. This literature review provided a foundation for our understanding of the history and existing state of play in human aspects of military operations.

We then conducted interviews with subject-matter experts (SMEs) and key stakeholders to better understand what and how human-domain-related efforts currently are incorporated into training, skill sets, and planning and operations within the Air Force, the broader U.S. Joint Force, and the militaries of two high-end allies, the UK and Germany. This involved semistructured interviews of 204 SMEs in 66 individual or group discussions; and included officials from training, specialty, and operational organizations throughout the services and partner militaries. These interviews were held between November 2017 and July 2018. We provide more details on these interviews in Appendix A, including an outline of topic areas and questions posed to interlocutors—developed based on the four research questions above—and a list of organizations and specialties interviewed as well as numbers of interviewees in each discussion.

Based on our literature review and insights from the SME interviews, we consolidated findings addressing the research questions and developed recommendations for how to better incorporate human-focused considerations into Air Force strategic planning and how to develop the necessary capabilities to enable successful operations.

Organization of the Report

The remaining chapters in this report document the study findings and recommendations. Chapter 2 examines the precedent and need for a new human domain. Chapter 3 describes various aspects of Air Force operations that involve human-focused capabilities and identifies institutional challenges to fully incorporating them into service functions. Chapter 4 explores approaches for considering and developing human aspects in operations already employed by other U.S. military services and selected partner-nation militaries. Chapter 5 examines the current gaps and opportunities within training and education to develop human-focused capabilities, including in models and wargaming. Finally, Chapter 6 summarizes the principal recommendations for how the Air Force can better incorporate consideration of human aspects into Air Force strategic planning and operations. As mentioned above, Appendix A provides background and details on the methodology we used to conduct the research reported here. Appendix B provides an overview of definitions and key characteristics of warfighting domains and discusses the extent to which these elements are consistent with the conceptualization of a human domain.

2. Precedent and Need for a Human Domain

As a component of the study reported herein, the Air Force asked RAND to assess whether there is a need for a new warfighting domain—a human domain. To explore this idea, this chapter assesses the extent to which there is a precedent and need for establishing a joint warfighting human domain as well as alternatives to that construct. In the sections below, we review previous efforts focused on incorporating sociocultural understanding into military operations, and describe key findings from our interviews with key stakeholders designed to gather strategic perspectives on whether or not there should be a sixth joint warfighting domain to encompass human aspects of military operations. We also examined characteristics of currently established warfighting domains (which include the land, maritime, air, space, and cyber domains) to assess their applicability to the establishment of a human-focused domain. We review findings from that analysis in more detail in Appendix B.

Recent Precedents for Establishing a Separate Warfighting Domain

Numerous efforts have been undertaken to incorporate cultural understanding into military operations in the United States, from anthropologists employed during World War II (Price, 2002) to the Human Terrain System through which civilian social scientists were deployed to Afghanistan and Iraq during Operations Enduring Freedom and Iraqi Freedom, respectively (McFate and Laurence, 2015). Further, publications by the Joint Chiefs of Staff such as *Joint Intelligence Preparation of the Operational Environment* (JP 2-01.3, 2014), *Counterinsurgency* (JP 3-24, 2018c), and *Stability* (JP 3-07, 2016) all include explicit consideration of cultural and social information in operations.[1] For the Air Force, understanding how this concept of human aspects of military operations impacts its air, space, and cyber operations and how to integrate human-focused capabilities into its planning, training, and even service culture could offer a more collaborative, synchronized, and integrated joint campaign approach to future conflicts focused on influencing adversary, neutral, and friendly audiences. Here, we introduce recent U.S. military treatment of the human-domain concept; more detailed information on joint and service doctrine can be found in Chapter 4.

The idea of developing a separate warfighting domain in this area—a human domain—received increased attention in 2013, when the Chief of Staff of the Army, GEN Raymond Odierno, the Marine Corps Commandant, Gen James Amos, and the Commander, U.S. Special Operations Command (USSOCOM), ADM William McRaven released *Strategic Landpower: Winning the Clash of Wills*. This white paper considered whether to adopt the term "human

---

[1] An extensive list of doctrinal publications can be found in Appendix A.

domain" as a doctrinal term along with its organizational, training, and other institutional implications. USSOCOM then incorporated the concept of a human domain into special operations guidance in 2015 with the publication of *Operating in the Human Domain*.

Both the strategic landpower white paper and the USSOCOM concept paper argued that a human domain should encompass the "physical, cultural, and social environments" of a broad array of conventional and other types of military operations (Odierno, Amos, and McRaven, 2013, p. 1) and should be a formal joint warfighting domain alongside land, sea, air, cyber, and space. However, that concept never became a predominant one, particularly as cultural competence and knowledge became "branded as an irregular warfare thing" that quickly fell out of favor once the wars in Iraq and Afghanistan drew down (Connable, 2018).

Throughout this time, other frameworks for incorporating human-domain-type capabilities into military operations have also emerged, including one developed by Army Special Operations Forces (ARSOF) that considers the full spectrum of warfare as an attempt to influence the cognitive (mental), affective (emotional), and physical aspects of a target audience. Special operations SMEs we engaged contended that a human domain could account for all three of these aspects; however, influencing the cognitive and affective realms in particular is most directly tied to and reliant on understanding the social and cultural environment of that audience. If war is ultimately an attempt to influence an opponent or competitor, knowing what the appropriate and most effective levers are—whether kinetic or nonkinetic in nature—is essential to success (author discussions with AFSOC and ARSOF officials, Fort Bragg, N.C., April 2018). These officials indicated that this approach is particularly relevant when considering the current focus on near-peer adversaries with whom the United States is in a state of extended competition rather than outright conflict. Understanding the human element is essential for operating in this competitive space, as it is far more efficient to understand the target audience fully before spending resources trying to influence it. And the human element is no less important in more open, direct conflict (Astorino-Courtois, 2017).

The JC-HAMO, while not advocating for a separate warfighting domain, identifies four imperatives that are critical to "updating" the mindset of the Joint Force to fully incorporate human aspects in military operations:

- *Identify* the range of relevant actors and their associated social, cultural, political, economic, and organizational networks.
- *Evaluate* relevant actor behavior in context.
- *Anticipate* relevant actor decisionmaking.
- *Influence* the will and decisions of relevant actors. (JC-HAMO, 2016, p. 2)

Further, these imperatives "apply to all facets of the National Military Strategy and all primary missions of the U.S. Armed Forces," including those of the U.S. Air Force (USAF), and "pertain to the full range of military operations . . . and the entire conflict spectrum" (JC-HAMO, 2016, p. 2). As such, the JC-HAMO itself emphasizes the encompassing nature of human aspects and establishes its relevance to high-order warfighting as well as counterinsurgency, counterterrorism, and steady-state peacetime operations.

Thus, there is past and current recognition of the importance of incorporating the human element explicitly into military operations, including some consideration as to whether a new warfighting domain should be developed. However, as described above, previous efforts for a more focused warfighting domain in this area have not gained traction. Still, there is a need to refocus on human aspects of military operations and to consider the possibility of establishing a human domain in a way that recognizes past efforts—and continuing obstacles.

Is a Human Domain Needed?

The strongest advocates for developing a formal human domain whom we engaged with were members of the joint special operations community who, as mentioned above, already have a concept paper dedicated to the subject (United States Special Operations Command, 2015). The individuals we spoke with stressed that capabilities related to the human domain historically have been subject to the ebb and flow of interest (and resources) from the services. They argued that resources dedicated to developing and maintaining these capabilities are often the first to be cut by the services in times of budget reductions or downsizing because they are often seen as lower priority than maintaining readiness in primary service domains of operation (such as the air domain for the Air Force). Additionally, the effects of human-focused capabilities are more difficult to measure than warfighting capabilities, and therefore related capabilities are more vulnerable because they cannot be "racked-and-stacked" against other capabilities for purposes of prioritization.

For example, after the drawdowns in Iraq and Afghanistan, Army civil affairs cadres were reduced in size from two full brigades to one brigade and a supplementary battalion, despite an increasingly demanding mission set in and, importantly, beyond those countries. In such times, interviewees said, it becomes routine to leave human considerations to others external to conventional force structure—Special Operations Forces (SOF), the Department of State, and other interagency partners—who do not have the capacity to provide support everywhere it is needed. Our special operations interlocutors noted that large-scale wargames illustrate this point, with human-domain elements not an intrinsic part of the game (see Chapter 5 on wargaming for more detail corroborating this point). Many of these interviewees stressed that having a clear, separable domain and associated proponent for human-domain capabilities would ensure that these skills and lessons do not atrophy in the face of changing strategic missions (AFSOC officials).

Our interlocutors outside the special operations community tended to agree that it is important to emphasize and ensure that the U.S. military develop human-focused capabilities; however, they were less certain that creating a new warfighting domain was the best way to do so. Among them, a common refrain was as follows: Humans are in all the domains—they are the central domain. Without humans, there would be no warfare in the first place, which theorists like Sun Tzu were writing about thousands of years ago. How could you separate them out?

Some interviewees expressed concern that if the human domain were formalized, it would mean that the services would abdicate responsibility for considering and developing their own capabilities along those lines but would realistically continue to need them. Instead, they felt, it would be more important for each service to recognize its own need for such capabilities and develop them, even if done (and in some cases, preferably done) in concert with each other.

Interlocutors at service educational and doctrinal institutions like Air University and the Army John F. Kennedy Special Warfare Center and School took a broader theoretical perspective. They contended that with the trends in modern competition and warfare, the concept of discrete domains is becoming outdated, so rather than adding a new domain, human considerations should be the cornerstone of a broader reenvisioning of multi-domain operations. Other interviewees raised more practical concerns. The reality, they said, is that a new domain requires new resources that have to come from somewhere else. With funding already constrained across the Department of Defense (DoD), they felt it unlikely that even domain proponents would support a reallocation of resources to stand up a new domain.

As we discuss in more detail in Appendix B, our review of what constitutes a warfighting domain highlighted that there is neither an agreed-on, documented, doctrinal definition of a warfighting domain nor an agreed-on delineation of the characteristics of warfighting domains, more broadly (Cornelius, 2015). This lack of clearly identified and commonly accepted characteristics of warfighting domains appears to contribute some confusion to debates regarding the recognition of new domains.

In light of the doctrinal uncertainty about the definition of a joint warfighting domain and whether it might apply to the human element, fairly widespread hesitation about the theoretical need for a distinct human domain among SMEs and stakeholders we interviewed, and the pragmatic constraints on resources that would make formally establishing a new domain challenging, we conclude that developing a separate human domain at this time is not advantageous. However, as required by the JC-HAMO and as we illustrate in the remaining chapters of this report, there is a strong need for the services to develop and maintain human-domain-type capabilities. While this may seem obvious for the primarily land-based services, it is no less true for the Air Force, across a broad spectrum of operations.

With this context in mind, for the purposes of this report we eschew the term "human domain" and instead focus on "human aspects of military operations." In keeping with the spirit of the JC-HAMO characterization of the concept quoted in Chapter 1, *we define "human aspects" as the social, cultural, political, and human knowledge as well as cross-cultural competency skills that are essential to and enhance the effectiveness of military operations.* Other institutions and organizations use separate terms for this concept, including "human terrain," "human dimension," "cognitive and affective domains," "human factors," and others; in this report, we incorporate all these concepts under the umbrella of human aspects of military operations.

Incorporation of Human Aspects in the Application of Air, Space, and Cyber Power

In light of our conclusion that establishing a separate, formal human domain is unwarranted, we instead focus on helping the Air Force consider how and why it should leverage the JC-HAMO to develop organic human-aspects capabilities. Developing these capabilities should not be and does not have to be at the expense of developing expertise in airpower, cyber, and space. The JC-HAMO emphasizes that all echelons of the Joint Force need a "foundational understanding" of human aspects; likewise, we argue that all airmen should be exposed at a basic level to the human aspects of military operations and, indeed, that it should become part of Air Force culture. Moreover, we find that human-focused capabilities should be selectively developed at different levels for different functional areas where airmen need

- to understand the strategic role human aspects can play in planning and assessing campaigns and operations
- to have in-depth knowledge of certain societies and cultures in order to inform their inputs into the decisionmaking and planning processes
- to develop cross-cultural skills that enable them to work with host nation populations and military partners.

However, unlike other models that look to outsource these capabilities (e.g., the Human Terrain System) or to centralize them (e.g., within Special Operations units), we suggest that developing this knowledge and skill set in a more planned and coordinated effort throughout the Air Force will provide the greatest benefit for operations and for the JC-HAMO goal of "updating the mindset" of the Joint Force.

Human Aspects: An Air Force Equity?

That the application of airpower can have effects on a population well beyond immediate tactical destruction of a target has been well documented. Air campaigns have had enormous psychological effects on populations and enemy combatants. The need to understand and take full advantage of those effects in a campaign or operation—rather than underutilizing such a capability or, worse, creating unintended effects—is compelling. Such effects should be an explicit part of Air Force planning, decisionmaking, operations, and analysis (Hosmer, 1996).

The viewpoint that the human aspects of military operations is an Air Force equity was widely supported across the Air Force stakeholders we interviewed. Many interlocutors felt strongly that from the strategic to the tactical levels, the Air Force needs more systematic thinking about and approaches to the human aspect of warfare in multi-domain operations, particularly in the air, cyber, and even space domains in which the Air Force takes a leading role. Some of the specifics of the kinds of operations and planning processes that might benefit most from increased understanding of the human element of warfare are discussed in Chapter 3. But overall, many interlocutors felt that if the military is not taking into consideration sociocultural understandings and how to influence people, it has lost sight of the fact that warfare is intrinsically a human endeavor, and without such considerations the military will never maximize its effectiveness.

Some interviewees did question why human aspects should be the military's or, more specifically, the Air Force's responsibility. In a whole-of-government approach, they maintained, the State Department should be leading this effort. Or, in a few cases, individuals argued that a combatant commander should be the one considering the desired effect on a given target population or force and how to best achieve it. The Air Force, by this view, is only responsible for carrying out its pieces of the plan, not for thinking about the consequences.

Other discussants argued that this perspective is shortsighted. They suggested that for numerous operations, the Air Force is the primary or only service employed, and if it lacks the organic capabilities to plan and assess operations from this effects-oriented angle, their missions will be less successful. For example, one interlocutor put it, "Understanding human aspects is a powerful force multiplier. Why would we take it off the table because we only do 'air stuff'?" (Author discussions with Headquarters Air Force [HAF] officials, Washington, D.C., May 2018.) In addition, if the Air Force lacks its own capabilities in this arena, it will have to rely on other services or on SOF such as the Army's Psychological Operations or Civil Affairs units to provide such insight. According to one interviewee, relying on the capabilities of other organizations is problematic, because "it's about their priorities—the Air Force is never going to get a PsyOp team to protect an air base if the Army isn't located there. Their units are limited, and we're at the bottom of their priority list" (author discussions with AFSOC officials, Hurlburt Field, Fla., May 2018).

Air Force intelligence and information operations (IO) officials also argued that no one outside the service understands the full range of Air Force capabilities as well as its own airmen. Relying on the State Department or a combatant commander to make the best decisions about which platforms to utilize and how to produce the intended outcomes may result in inappropriate use of airpower. By contrast, if the Air Force component has a strong understanding of what the intended effects are for a given operation or campaign combined with a knowledge of the human environment they are operating in, they may be able to make suggestions that increase the efficacy of air, cyber, or space power (author discussions with HAF officials, Washington, D.C., May 2018).[2]

An Important Prerequisite to Airmen's Success in Joint Positions

This joint perspective is important in multiple ways. Interviewees explained that, when working in joint positions or on country teams that involve interaction with interagency colleagues, Air Force personnel suddenly become responsible for helping make these kinds of decisions at the strategic level. If they are not prepared to do so through education, training, and experience, they are less effective in these positions. Some non–Air Force interlocutors with backgrounds in the human aspects of military operations observed inconsistency in the human-

---

[2] Previous RAND research has looked at the importance of understanding human behavior from an intelligence, surveillance, and reconnaissance (ISR) perspective, particularly when the United States has fewer forces on the ground (and thus less ability to obtain human intelligence). See Cragin et al., 2017.

aspects knowledge of Air Force personnel in joint positions. Although they had worked with some Air Force personnel who understood the human environment and its importance at the strategic, operational, and tactical levels, they stated that most were inadequately prepared to think in these ways and so, according to these interlocutors, were less successful than their sister-service counterparts.

Given concerns about relatively low Air Force representation in joint positions, Chief of Staff of the Air Force Gen David Goldfein has set one of his major goals as developing airmen to be better prepared to serve in joint positions (Losey, 2016). Ensuring that Air Force personnel have a broader and deeper understanding of the role of the human environment and its relation to operations and strategy is, according to some of our interviewees, one way to develop airmen to serve in these positions. Similarly, a recent study examining how to improve Air Force representation in joint senior leader positions recommends that officers receive more education in the specific geographic regions in which they hope to do future joint assignments to help enhance their strategic thinking in a joint capacity (Lee et al., 2017).

Applying the JC-HAMO Framework in the Air Force

Fortunately, the JC-HAMO offers a construct for operationalizing such human considerations that the Air Force can apply. It provides a detailed outline of the kinds of capabilities required to effectively conduct military operations that take human considerations into account (Joint Chiefs of Staff, 2018a). This is in conjunction with two additional joint concepts, the *Joint Concept for Operating in the Information Environment*, which focuses on "leveraging the inherent informational aspects of military activities to affect the perceptions, attitudes, and other elements that drive desired behaviors through the integration of physical and information power [understanding the fight we face and understanding the impact of our actions on the fight]" (Joint Chiefs of Staff, 2018b, p. 1), and the *Joint Concept for Integrated Campaigning*, which is defined as "Joint Force and interorganizational partner efforts to enable the achievement and maintenance of policy aims by integrating military activities and aligning non-military activities of sufficient scope, scale, simultaneity, and duration across multiple domains" (Joint Chiefs of Staff, 2018a, p. 6). Together, these concepts provide a framework for more effectively utilizing and engaging the human environment to achieve desired effects.

The Air Force can draw from these developing joint concepts to inculcate its airmen across the force with an understanding of the human aspects of military operations. As the JC-HAMO states, all echelons of the Joint Force should have foundational knowledge of human aspects, but more advanced human-focused capabilities might be required in certain organizations, career fields, and positions. Chapter 3 explores a range of Air Force mission sets that would benefit from having this more advanced level of human-focused capabilities, assesses the current level of these capabilities in Air Force mission and functional areas and related training and education, and identifies challenges to developing the full depth of knowledge and skills necessary to successfully operate in the human environment.

3. Current Status of Human-Focused Capabilities in the U.S. Air Force

Consideration of human aspects is incorporated extensively in the USAF's special operations community, but to a lesser degree within the conventional Air Force. Some conventional Air Force activities, from development of the information operations career field to a nascent recognition of the human aspects of space and cyber missions, have begun to focus on human elements in their mission sets. However, the concept of human aspects of military operations is not systematically institutionalized across the conventional Air Force, and gaps exist between current capabilities and potential needs; in addition, limitations in training exist. In the first section below, we begin a discussion of these challenges by reviewing AFSOC's approach to human-focused capabilities. Then, in subsequent sections, we turn to the conventional Air Force by exploring the degree to which human aspects are recognized in five relevant mission areas: strategic and operational planning, intelligence, security cooperation (SC), cyberspace, and space. We also review a few smaller mission areas that require such consideration. Later, in Chapter 5, we explore concepts for inculcating all echelons of the Air Force with a foundational understanding of human aspects, as put forth in the JC-HAMO.

Air Force Special Operations

As a special operations organization, AFSOC makes heavy use of the special operations operating concept, which includes a focus on developing a better understanding of human aspects "to identify and influence relevant actors to produce outcomes acceptable to the U.S." (USSOCOM, 2016, p. 1). Not every element of AFSOC has the need for specialized knowledge or skills in the human-aspects arena, but some specialties, namely, battlefield airmen (combat controllers, pararescue, tactical air control, and special operations weather career fields) and Combat Aviation Advisors (CAAs), engage with foreign cultures at the tactical level and so have a strong need for capabilities related to understanding human aspects of military operations. We provide background on both these specialties below.

Human Aspects in Special Operations

Battlefield airman is a special operations skill set that requires advanced understanding of human aspects of military operations. Battlefield airmen are often embedded with land forces in order to facilitate the use of airpower. Whereas weather-oriented airmen will have input into operational planning, most battlefield airmen have a need for tactical cross-cultural communication skills and local cultural knowledge rather than an emphasis on the role of human aspects in planning.

13

CAAs, however, need an element of both. Like conventional Air Advisors, CAAs spend much of their time deployed to partner nations to help train, advise, and assist in developing partner air force capabilities. However, they do so much more intensively, often returning consistently to the same nations to build capacity as well as relationships. Unlike conventional advisors, they present a small footprint, and in conflict zones CAAs may also be authorized to actively assist their partners in missions. CAAs, then, not only need the tactical-level cultural knowledge and skills, but also need to be ready to consider the human aspects of planning at the operational level (if assisting in a mission with a partner nation) and the strategic level (as they make long-term plans for appropriately and effectively developing partner capabilities). Specifically, CAAs need knowledge of the human aspects of the general population as well as of the institutional culture of a partner nation's military (AFSOC officials).

Human-Aspects-Related Training in Special Operations

As a specialized set of units, AFSOC has its own training and education regimens designed to fully endow its personnel with the human-aspects skills and knowledge they need in their mission.[1] Battlefield airmen undergo an extensive training environment prior to being accepted into the career field. CAA, on the other hand, is not an explicit career field, but a specialty an airman can volunteer to join after a certain amount of time in the Air Force. In addition to a 12- to 18-month training cycle that includes extensive cultural knowledge and skills provided by the USAF Special Operations School, CAAs undergo a rigorous selection process that ensures they meet certain physical, psychological, and emotional requirements. As a result, the average age and maturity level of CAAs are higher than for the Air Force more broadly, and individuals who are not well suited for engaging intensively with partner-nation personnel are not selected (AFSOC officials).

AFSOC Challenges

However, AFSOC's focus on human aspects of military operations is not without its challenges. For example, as with many other actors who engage in human aspects of military operations, AFSOC interviewees said they struggle with developing and providing easily quantifiable measures of effect: "The hard thing is you can't measure the effects of what we do, and the Air Force doesn't like things that can't be measured. You can measure when there has been a disaster, but it's impossible to measure when one has been avoided, or to say exactly why" (author discussions with AFSOC officials, Hulburt Field, Fla., October 2017).

In another example of challenges, CAAs do a single tour and then revert back to their primary specialty in the conventional Air Force. The extensive training pipeline means that

---

[1] It was beyond the scope of the current study to conduct an evaluation of the effectiveness of this training and education.

airmen often are only operational CAAs for two and a half to three years, creating a heavy training bill for AFSOC.

Another major challenge AFSOC faces in its focus on human aspects is integrating with the conventional Air Force. According to one AFSOC representative:

> It's like they decided that human domain is a special operations thing and not their problem. We go to wargames and exercises, and they sprinkle in a little human domain to give us something to do, but it's not a part of Big Air Force's planning or thinking for the rest of what they're doing. We're not included in that. (Author discussions with AFSOC officials, Hurlburt Field, Fla., October 2017)

When we asked what could be done to make this situation better, interviewees suggested that better informing Air Force senior leaders both about CAA capabilities and about the importance of thinking about a range of kinetic and nonkinetic solutions would be important. They argued that things like battle damage assessments should consider not just the analysis of the targets, but the analysis of the secondary effects on the local population.

Overall, training for and preparation to engage in the human aspects of military operations is much more prevalent and in depth in the Air Force special operations community. However, retaining those capabilities and integrating them and the human-aspects knowledge AFSOC brings to bear into the conventional forces provide ongoing challenges for both AFSOC and the broader Air Force.

In the sections below, we now turn to exploring the degree to which human aspects is recognized within the conventional Air Force in five relevant mission areas: strategic and operational planning, intelligence, SC, cyberspace, and space. We also review a few smaller mission areas that require such consideration.

Strategic and Operational Planning

In our exploration of human aspects in strategic and operational planning and more generally as part of our study, RAND team members attended the USAF's Global Engagement wargame—a preeminent exercise of strategists and planners, among others—to examine how human aspects of military operations were being incorporated into Air Force wargaming and analysis. Overall, the RAND team made two telling observations about the role of human aspects in military operations while watching the planning cell in action. First, we noticed that on a map of the area under consideration the cell had drawn on a whiteboard, borders were drawn to indicate countries, and the map was covered in frequently redrawn symbols indicating home and opponent forces. What was entirely missing on the map were cities, which would be critical in being able to think strategically about how operations may affect the broader population in the region. Second, not once did we hear any consideration about what might actually be effective in making the opponent back down or cease combat operations. The planning cell, and the more senior strategic cell that was providing big-picture guidance, worked fluidly to plan conventional, joint operations, but did not stop to consider the efficacy of their operations in terms of achieving the ultimate aim of making the opponent withdraw.

It was notable that a game designed to exercise strategy and operational planning and the joint application of airpower failed to take human aspects into the development of courses of action or adjudication of outcomes. These human-aspects considerations are critical to being able to understand the potential impact of operations on the opponent's will to fight and decisionmaking. Human aspects, therefore, should be considered by airmen tasked to interpret a conflict environment and provide information to commanders—as well as by the commanders themselves, who must know the right questions to ask as part of their decisionmaking and must integrate human aspects of military operations into their plans.

IO is an increasingly important area of concern for strategic and operational planning. As one AFSOC representative we spoke with stated, "Every word, action, or inaction sends a message. We need to make sure that we're sending the message we mean to send and, even more importantly, that the audience is getting the message we mean to send and not something we didn't mean to say" (Author discussions with AFSOC officials, Hulburt Field, Fla., October 2017).

The Joint Chiefs of Staff have addressed this concern by calling for greater inclusion of the concept of information. In 2017, information was made the seventh joint warfighting function, along with command and control, intelligence, fires, movement and maneuver, protection, and sustainment. The definition they provide for this function is that it

> encompasses the management and application of information and its deliberate
> integration with other joint functions to influence relevant actor perceptions,
> behavior, action or inaction, and supports human and automated decision making.
> The information function helps commanders and staffs understand and leverage
> the pervasive nature of information, its military uses, and its application during all
> military operations. (JP 1, 2017, p. i–19)

The Joint Chiefs of Staff directed the services to stand up IO career fields to facilitate the inclusion of information into a wide range of military operations. The approach propels the idea that a strategic narrative developed in coordination with the interagency community will drive all engagements and operations with allies and competitors alike to ensure that the United States is sending a consistent message with its words and actions.

Human aspects play a central role in this process, as influencing behavior and decisionmaking relies heavily on understanding local social, cultural, and political contexts, as does knowing how to measure whether or not military actions or messages are having their intended cognitive and affective effects. Recognizing this need, the Air Force built out its officer-only IO career field with the requirement that officers have a degree in a behavioral or social science. Along with intelligence personnel (discussed later in this chapter), IO officers therefore stand to be the main locus for effectively incorporating human aspects into Air Force operations—both for traditional air campaigns and for integrated, multi-domain efforts that incorporate space, cyber, and even sea or land elements (HAF officials). Therefore, the remainder of this section is devoted to discussion of IO expertise.

Human Aspects in Operational Planning

IO positions are located in several places across the Air Force but are primarily concentrated in Air Operations Centers and reachback centers such as the National Air and Space Intelligence Center's (NASIC's) behavioral and social cell. In the Air Operations Centers, IO officers can provide input into how to craft strategic narratives, plan operations that align with those narratives, craft specific messages as stand-alone pieces or as part of other operations, and find opportunities to measure the impact of all the operations on the intended audiences. At NASIC, in conjunction with civilian support, these officers can provide support to any element as well as regional expertise on various countries, regions, or populations. In these positions, they can help planners and commanders consider how to do everything from using social media campaigns to helping understand the military culture of an opponent and what the most efficient way to influence military or political decisionmakers using military means might be.

IO officers, though, face several challenges in playing these roles effectively. One is that they are relatively small in number. With only about 200 officers, they often are not incorporated in all the places they could be. For instance, it has been suggested that IO officers would be better utilized in the planning or operations cells at the major commands, where they could be more integrated into a wider array of planning, rather than primarily in the Air Operations Centers (U.S. Air Forces in Europe [USAFE] officials). Another challenge is that the career field is fairly new. Though elements in the Air Force previously performed similar activities, until 2016 they were not consistently combined into a single career field that developed expertise in all of the various activities that IO might encompass (Losey, 2018). As such, these activities were applied on an ad hoc basis at best, and the result has been that many non-IO personnel do not understand what IO is or what capabilities it really brings to bear.

In our interviews, IO officers across the services, and even similar officers in partner-nation militaries (see Chapters 4 and 5), declared that rather than being a part of the planning cycle up front, they are often treated as an afterthought, asked to create messages that support operations instead of being an integral piece of considering where and how to develop operations in the first place. As one IO officer stated, "It's an organizational and a cultural problem. They don't know how or where to use us and don't care to when they do" (author discussions with HAF official, Washington, D.C., January 2018). That sentiment is not universal, though, as many IO officers (as well as Civil Affairs and Psychological Operations personnel in the Army) said it can be very personality dependent, with some commanders and planners understanding the importance of human aspects and others not—begging the question of what exposure these commanders and planners have had to human aspects of military operations. They also observed that senior leaders often seem to be more convinced of the importance of human aspects, but that the roadblock is often with the midcareer officers involved in planning who have not had as much experience in planning and leading operations. This disparity, then, suggests that while there is individual buy-in, the importance of IO and of human aspects in military operations has not yet been institutionalized in the education, culture, or mindset of the Air Force.

A final challenge raised during our interviews is contending with a military mindset that requires clear measures of effectiveness for operations. Many of the effects that do fall within the purview of IO and rely heavily on engaging in human aspects are qualitative in nature and not easy to measure, and the impact often takes a relatively long period of time to manifest. Although there may be some avenues for measuring effects such as using social media, changes in attitudes and behavior may take a long time to become visible, or, alternatively, they may be highly volatile and difficult to attribute to specific efforts. They also require expertise in the local language, locally preferred social media venues, and a baseline to compare against. And sometimes when the intended effect is something like preventing violence, there are almost no options for measurement, given that measuring a negative is universally problematic. Given these challenges, the Air Force IO officers we spoke with worried that their contributions would be less valued and their careers less promising because of the complex nature of their work. Research has illuminated means of measuring efforts to inform, influence, and persuade, providing some insight into how to address these challenges (e.g., Paul et al., 2015). Furthermore, developing measures of effectiveness that consider human aspects, that are qualitative, and that are long term should be essential for all operations to make sure they are having the intended effect in more than just the near future.

Human-Aspects-Related Training in Information Operations

The IO technical training schoolhouse was in the process of standing up at the time of this study. Prior to its development, IO officers borrowed curricula from a variety of sister services and joint courses on topics like military information support activities, electronic warfare, and military deception (Losey, 2018). Officers we spoke with in this career field stressed that skills like cross-cultural communication, perspective taking, and emotional intelligence are also essential for what they do, as such skills enable them to more effectively understand and operate in the human environment across different cultures and societies. They noted that there is tension, though, between the need for practitioners who have these types of skills and the need for regional expertise that enables an IO officer to apply them effectively in a particular social or cultural context. Although reachback centers like NASIC can provide some of that expertise, they are limited in size, and the officers themselves lack the time to become regional experts because their career trajectories can take them to any region and so require them to be experts at their craft instead. During our interviews, this tension was echoed by sister and partner nation services and even other Air Force career fields such as cyber. There is no clear answer to this challenge, though options might include building a complementary enlisted career field that develops regional specialties, making use of a reserve force or increased civilian reachback expertise, or aligning officers to particular regions more explicitly to allow them to develop expertise.

Operational Planning Challenges

Despite the high-level mandate to develop an IO capability in each service, our interviews highlighted several challenges to the effective use and development of this capability within the Air Force. Better recognition from the highest to lowest echelons regarding the importance and relevance of IO in all strategic and operational planning, more robust incorporation of IO into the operations and planning cycles, and more specialized training and education would all serve to improve the Air Force's ability to operate in the information and human aspects of warfare.

Intelligence

In a joint operations environment, Air Force intelligence analysts play a critical role in providing relevant information and assessments to support mission accomplishment. Several responsibilities shape this role: informing the commander; describing the operational environment; identifying, defining, and nominating objectives; supporting planning and execution of operations; countering adversary deception and surprise; supporting friendly deception effort;[2] and assessing the effectiveness of operations (JP 2-0, 2013, p. ix). When addressing the human aspect of military operations from the intelligence analyst's perspective, two avenues of analytical approach come to mind: (1) analysis of adversarial personalities, networks, groups, and their cultural environments, and (2) analysis of the populations in which the adversary exists.

The former approach emphasizes understanding the adversary, first and foremost, not through its orders of battle or technological achievements but through its people and their capacity and desire either to wage war or to abstain from it. The latter approach, on the other hand, explores specific pockets within the observable population that have already shown propensity toward aggression against the United States and its allies or partners, and their level of influence on the surrounding population and state leadership. Both analyses are important in conventional and unconventional conflicts and are described in joint and Air Force–specific intelligence operations doctrine (see Air Force Doctrine Document [AFDD] 2-0, 2012, and JP 2-0, 2013). However, despite the criticality of human aspects in both types of conflict, doctrine places much greater emphasis on the unconventional—namely, intelligence support to IO and irregular warfare—and on the adversary when it comes to prioritizing analysis of the human aspects of the operational picture.

Based on our interviews, commanders' intelligence requirements tend to favor adversary threat-based military capabilities. These requirements are easier to fulfill and have clear objectives and measurable effects. Requirements that address the human aspects of military

---

[2] "Altering the perception of an adversary—to mislead or delude—helps achieve security and surprise. Intelligence and counterintelligence (CI) support effective friendly information operations (IO) through sociocultural analysis (SCA) of adversary leadership characteristics" (JP 2-0, 2013, p. I-4).

operations, on the other hand, involve cognitive analyses that are more difficult to perform, often do not present clear objectives, and can lead to either unquantifiable effects or effects that may only be observed over prolonged periods of time. For these reasons, intelligence requirements that rely on analysis of the human aspects of military operations are less prevalent, hold lower priority, and are fulfilled using limited resources.

Human Aspects in Intelligence Support to Information Operations

Intelligence analysts focus on human aspects most closely when supporting an IO mission in the course of friendly deception efforts. Analysts conduct predictive analysis of adversary intentions and derive adversary potential courses of action (COAs) through the processes of intelligence preparation of the operational environment (IPOE) and understanding the political, military, economic, social, infrastructure, and information context. The ultimate goal is to identify the most effective COAs to inform military actions at all levels of war.[3]

These analysts' assessments are usually threat-based or population-based, with the latter derived from an analysis of human aspects termed "sociocultural analysis" in support of the IO mission (JP 2-0, 2013, p. I-4). The 2013 Joint publication *Joint Intelligence* defines social-cultural analysis as "the analysis of adversaries and other relevant actors that integrates concepts, knowledge, and understanding of societies, populations, and other groups of people, including their activities, relationships, and perspectives across time and space at varying scales" (JP 2-0, 2013, p. GL-11). It identifies sociocultural analysis as "the most important, but least understood [aspect] of analysis" in joint intelligence preparation of the operational environment (JP 2-0, 2013, p. I-17).

Sociocultural knowledge is considered a beneficial skill for an intelligence analyst, but not one that is attached to a formal requirement or is standardized across a career field with a culture that emphasizes effects-based military operations (Author discussions with AFSOC officials, Hurlburt Field, Fla., October 2017). Rather, the training and daily routines of intelligence analysts are geared toward maximizing the kinetic effects of Air Force operations, for which sociocultural understanding may be applied in a limited way and with limited success. There is greater emphasis on threat-based analysis of "standard order-of-battle factors" like the composition, disposition, strength, tactics, techniques, and procedures of adversary forces. In certain operations involving the targeting of key actors and high-value targets, however, sociocultural analysis is critical to identifying and tracking them.

Due to the recent counterterrorism and counterinsurgency efforts in Iraq, Afghanistan, and elsewhere, sociocultural analysis has been associated most commonly with intelligence support in irregular warfare—where the strategic focus is to gain and maintain influence over and support

---

[3] AFPAM 14-118, *Aerospace Intelligence Preparation of the Battlespace*, dated 2001, was rescinded and has not yet been replaced. Air Force Intelligence analysts currently use JP 2-01.3, *Joint Intelligence Preparation of the Operational Environment* (2014), for guidance on the IPOE process.

of the relevant population (JP 2-01.3, 2014, p. VII-2). In this case, the population constitutes the very environment in which military forces conduct operations. Application of the IPOE process to irregular warfare involves more focus on the sociocultural aspects of the adversary and the civilians among whom he operates. The role of the intelligence analyst, then, is to anticipate obstacles to fulfilling the joint mission by defining the operational environment in which the population may either welcome or resist outside assistance (JP 2-01.2, 2014, p. 168).

Intelligence analysts conduct human intelligence (HUMINT) collection and analysis, which is critical to supporting IO in irregular warfare. Irregular adversaries are often embedded in local societies and live undetected within self-forming networks with constantly changing nodes among the population (Annex 3-2, 2016, p. 4, and Annex 2-0, 2015, p. 41). HUMINT collectors will use local sources and host or partner nation networks to help engage with the local population more easily through debriefings, interrogations, and source operations (Pawlyk, 2015, and HAF officials). Some results of these efforts may include pattern-of-life analyses and a map of the human factors that includes data on tribal relationships within a network of persons of interest. Intelligence sharing, as much as intelligence gathering, is key during intelligence support to irregular warfare and may require knowledge of both the language and culture of the surrounding population for these intelligence activities to be successful.

Just as important as collecting intelligence data on potential threat networks is friendly forces' ability to manage adversary or host nation perception of U.S. efforts in the area. The adversary is expected to run an IO campaign of his own, and countering that campaign is another HUMINT priority (Annex 3-2, 2016, p. 4). Intelligence analysts have to anticipate the population's response to friendly operations in the course of irregular operations and monitor indicators of socioeconomic and cultural stressors. Managing the social, political, and economic consequences may be the difference between deciding to apply lethal military force or making social or economic improvements in a key area.

The overall target development process applies analysis and products developed during IPOE to identify potential targets, like financial markets or the media, suitable for nonkinetic effects. Targeting vulnerability assessments then helps to identify adversary target vulnerabilities to DoD nonkinetic capabilities. Behavioral analysis of a person or entity-level target further assesses the adversary's "vulnerability, susceptibility and accessibility" to DoD influence operations (363rd *Intelligence Surveillance Reconnaissance Group Operating Instruction*, 2016, and JP 2-0, 2013, I-19).

In 2015, the 17th Intelligence Squadron at Joint Base Langley-Eustis in Virginia gained the mission to support so-called nonkinetic targeting effects. The squadron comprises a mix of intelligence and IO analysts who work on cyber effects, influence operations, effects in the electromagnetic spectrum, cognitive target development, and behavioral analysis. Such effects are often difficult to quantify, however, our interviewees noted. How, for example, do you measure the impact on thoughts in a target population, or stop someone from conducting beheadings without applying lethal military force (NASIC officials)?

Behavioral analysts recognize that to be more effective, they need to have a good understanding of the commander's objectives and of the stated operational desired and undesired effects. However, based on our interviews, we were told that often such analysts do not have insight into what U.S. military forces are trying to do and what their objectives are. For example, assessing the potential course of action of a person of interest based on behavioral analysis becomes more context-based than individual-based when objectives are unclear or undisclosed. With proper direction, however, the analytical focus can be not just on the individual profile, but also on how the target person might notice a particular U.S. action and divert their actions toward a desired U.S. effect (NASIC officials).

Although the behavioral analysis community is small and their mission well known, we were also informed that they find themselves continuously educating and reminding the operational community about their capabilities and about what they can provide for the operational community. Additionally, limited resources constantly drive them to prioritize their work based on current requirements, where the mindset to integrate with kinetics still largely persists.

Human-Aspects-Related Training in Intelligence Analysis

Recent RAND research suggests that ISR analysts are increasingly asked in irregular warfare environments to interpret the behavior they observe of adversaries, partner forces, and civilian populations in addition to the physical status of potential targets. The research concluded, however, that these analysts are insufficiently trained to provide appropriate insight into human behavior (Cragin et al., 2017).

In other areas of intelligence analysis, there is much more attention to developing human-focused capabilities. One of these is in HUMINT collection, which has been performed by Air Force intelligence analysts for many years but has only recently become a permanent Air Force specialty (HAF officials). New entrants into the field without prior intelligence training attend the Intelligence Fundamentals Course for approximately three weeks before proceeding to the Defense Strategic Debriefing Course (just over five weeks). Here, they learn general and cross-cultural communication skills, as well as how sociocultural information applies to HUMINT operations (HAF officials). Potential Air Force HUMINT operators possess the ability to assess people and their environment, to develop a rapport with their contacts, and to manipulate people. According to our interviewees, current training provides some exposure to foreign languages, but operators are expected to assess, debrief, and interrogate sources on any topic in English (HAF officials). Other specialty qualifications include mandatory knowledge of "human personality characteristics, traits, habits and behaviors" (*Air Force Enlisted Classification Directory* [AFECD], 2017). Once at the operational unit, HUMINT specialists undergo more localized training based on the unit's specific mission and qualification training derived from the HUMINT career field education and training plan (HAF officials).

Other intelligence disciplines that provide synergy to irregular warfare operations, aside from HUMINT, include geospatial and signals intelligence (Annex 3-2, 2016). The latter may require the application of cryptologic language analysis to collect, transcribe, translate, evaluate, analyze, and report relevant foreign language communications (AFECD, 2017). Even though acquiring this type of intelligence relies on technical collection means, understanding the cultural context that underlies their foreign language specialty allows cryptologic linguists to go beyond the literal translation of the collected intelligence. It is, in fact, the duty and responsibility of the cryptologic linguist "to convey the meaning of an activity or situation" and "to identify regional and cultural factors associated with activities of interest" (AFECD, 2017, p.67). Potential cryptologic language analysts do not have to have prior experience with a foreign language but do have to score well enough on the Defense Language Aptitude Battery or Oral Proficiency Interview to earn their Air Force specialty code (AFSC) following completion of a designated training curriculum at the Defense Language Institute (AFECD, 2017).

The existing formal training pipeline for the Air Force targeting intelligence career field follows an established approach from initial training through required qualification training through advanced training for both officers and enlisted professionals. A limited number of courses address intelligence support to information operations at the advanced level for officers. Supplemental and cross-functional training opportunities exist for both officers and enlisted personnel, but it is unclear how often Air Force targeting analysts get the opportunity to attend these courses.

Knowledge of some human aspects of Air Force military operations is considered a beneficial skill for an intelligence analyst but not one that is required for the performance of intelligence duties; threat-based analysis remains dominant. With the exception of cryptologic language analysts, no other Air Force intelligence AFSC requires formal language training. Cultural training is not a formal requirement, either, and regional training is limited to unit-specific operations and constrained by unit-level resources available to provide that training. While supplemental and cross-functional training opportunities exist, exposure to the effects of human aspects within the formal training pipeline is more prominent in more specialized training courses.

In sum, in our survey of consideration of human aspects in the USAF intelligence community, we found important areas where intelligence professionals incorporated this perspective in their activities. However, operational communities tend to lack the necessary background in human aspects that would enable them to ask relevant questions of the intelligence community. Early-career education about intelligence organizations that specialize to a greater extent in the human aspects, and the types of requirements they need to receive, might help raise the priority of human-focused capabilities. Likewise, intelligence analysts bound for organizations that specialize in human-aspects-based analysis do not receive the necessary formal education in this type of analysis prior to their arrival, to include relevant cultural or language training.

Security Cooperation

SC and working effectively with allies and partners is a major priority in the 2018 *National Defense Strategy* (DoD, 2018). The Chairman of the Joint Chiefs of Staff specifically called on the Air Force to play a significant role in developing partner nation air forces as part of maintaining alliances and partnerships (Secretary of the Air Force Public Affairs, 2017). SC activities support U.S. defense strategy by enhancing interoperability with key allies and partners, gaining and maintaining access and influence in regions vital to U.S. interests, building partner military and institutional capacity, enhancing the U.S. position vis-à-vis strategic competitors, and developing trusting partnerships.

While human-focused capabilities are a prominent feature of the training and experience of AFSOC's CAAs, understanding human aspects is an essential component for SC efforts that the conventional Air Force engages in, and across a broader spectrum than for some other types of activities. From the strategic to the tactical level, airmen who engage in SC need to understand the perspectives of the people they are working with, as well as those whom they are working against.

Human Aspects in Security Cooperation

At the most strategic level, SC is part of the suite of tools that the Air Force and the combatant commands apply to achieve intended outcomes in a region, and indeed globally. As with other planning efforts, airmen delivering SC need an understanding of how specific efforts to work with allies and partners are linked to effects, and how those efforts may need to be tailored to the local society and culture in order to have the most impact on adversaries, allies, or neutral audiences. SC planners and leaders need to understand the full range of effects SC provides to them, and its limitations. At the operational level, planners and implementers at Air Force component commands—such as USAFE, Air Force Africa (AFAFRICA), Pacific Air Forces, and others—need to have a strong understanding of the local popular and military institutional cultures in the various countries in their area of responsibility.

This expertise allows planners to translate strategic guidance from the Secretaries of State and Defense and the combatant commands into more practical plans for developing air-related partner capabilities that account for the particularities and limitations of a given country. For example, a desk officer planning for SC with Kenya would need to understand not only the baseline capabilities of the Kenyan Air Force, but also how willing the Kenyans are to work with the United States, what particular challenges exist in U.S. engagement with Kenya and its ability to absorb U.S. assistance, and what engagement would have the greatest effect in supporting U.S. and Kenyan interests. All of this requires some understanding of human aspects, including Kenyan history, social and political culture, interests, threats, and strategic outlook. While planning staffs are often too lightly manned to allow them to develop intensive knowledge of every country within their region, they can lean on country teams and the SC office located within U.S. embassies in partner capitals, although these teams may not always have an Air Force officer present and so may lack an Air Force perspective. Members of those country teams, along with individuals and teams tasked to provide training or serve as air advisors, require more tactical knowledge of a particular culture, as well as cross-cultural competence skills such as cross-cultural communication and negotiation techniques (USAFE officials).

SC includes a wide range of engagement activities, from foreign military sales and combined exercises, to training and education of foreign students, to planning conferences, to key-leader engagements and goodwill events. All require participating U.S. airmen to maintain various levels of understanding of partners' interests, institutional and societal cultures, and challenges, as well as their military capabilities. Training can either be formal training, such as that provided by the Inter-European Air Forces Academy (IEAFA)—a USAF-run academy that provides a Noncommissioned Officers Academy and Squadron Officers School to European and American airmen—or occur at the familiarization level, where U.S. airmen provide training, but the trainees do not receive any certification at the end. The major commands, Special Operations forces, the State Partnership Program—a program that partners Air National Guard units with allied countries—the Contingency Response Group, and Mobility Support and Advisory Squadrons (MSASs) all contribute to these trainings in various ways. Exercises may involve multiple units from several countries engaged in practicing several types of operations. Goodwill events may include things like medical outreach to local communities or performances by the USAF bands. All of these SC activities involve extensive planning and close engagement with allied and partner personnel, organizations, leaders, and communities, and require U.S. airmen to understand human aspects at various levels of competence.

Human-Aspects-Related Training in Security Cooperation

At the tactical level, there are three main sources of personnel with separate but related training pipelines in SC: Foreign Area Officers (FAOs), CAAs, and Air Advisors. FAOs often serve as part of embassy country teams and receive intensive training and education to qualify for their role, including language and regional familiarization training. This training is usually accompanied by an immersive education experience in a host country and a requirement to attend a degree program at some point that involves a regional focus. Unlike in the Army, the FAO track in the Air Force is not a full-time career field but is part of a dual-track system where officers alternate between FAO positions and positions in their original career field in order to keep them current with the operational force. CAAs are part of AFSOC squadrons focused on conducting the full range of advising roles in a wide range of environments, including austere, semipermissive ones. They undergo intensive physical and psychological screening before being accepted into the training regimen. The training they undertake at that point is heavily focused on cross-cultural skills, regional knowledge, and language, in addition to the training required to perform their specific roles.

25

Air Advisors are airmen in the conventional Air Force who volunteer or are tapped to perform advising missions in more permissive environments outside the special operations set. They may be assigned to one of two MSASs, which focus on South America or Africa, to a Contingency Response Group if they are selected for full tours, or they may fill individual advising positions deployed for up to a year to Iraq or Afghanistan as part of the continuing missions in those countries. Air Advisors in the MSAS receive fairly extensive training modeled on the CAA training, including a language requirement, while those going to a Contingency Response Group or deploying as individuals receive a week of language, region, and culture training just prior to leaving (Secretary of the Air Force, International Affairs (SAF/IA), USAFE, MSAS, and Air Advisor School officials).

There are a number of other tiers of airmen engaged in SC, including professionals in policy and planning roles, such as those in Air Force and Major Command headquarters and in implementing agencies like the Air Force Security Assistance Training (AFSAT) squadron and the Air Force Security Assistance and Cooperation (AFSAC) directorate. These professionals have various levels of training and experience through the Air Force and other organizations like the Defense Institute for Security Cooperation Studies. Moreover, many other airmen are tasked to work with allies and partners because of the functional skills they bring (e.g., maintenance, civil engineering, etc.), but may have very little background in regional or intercultural competencies.

Security Cooperation Challenges

Our interlocutors noted a number of challenges when it comes to incorporating human-aspects considerations into SC activities. The first is that there is an insufficient number of USAF personnel fully trained in SC, particularly those with the social and cultural competency to engage with foreign partners. Given the roles, responsibilities, and resources for each of these positions, training and education for some SC professionals like CAAs is quite strong and tailored to meet the needs of the airmen at a tactical level. The shortfall is instead in capacity, particularly for conventional Air Advisors and planners. According to the Air Advisor schoolhouse, the vast majority of their students are bound for Iraq and Afghanistan, leaving few students to focus on the other countries or regions. Most USAF personnel engaged in the State Partnership Programs receive little or no formal advisor training. The shortage of SC personnel is felt at the major commands, with component commands noting critically that the lack of air advisor–trained personnel on the staff or in the units limits their effectiveness (USAFE and AFAFRICA officials).

Second, one of the primary challenges SC practitioners face is in quantifying the effectiveness of their programs in meeting strategic aims. In some cases, the problem is time. If developing new capabilities or capacity for a partner nation is the goal, measuring how effective efforts have been at an institutional level takes far more time than an active-duty service member's tour. For building relations with partners, it is often suggested that sending a partner airman through

USAF schooling will pay off in the future when that airman becomes the head of their Air Force, remembers his or her time fondly, and so supports American forces. While we heard numerous anecdotes that these sorts of relations do pay off, they do so over the course of decades, making providing any concrete measures of effectiveness impossible for an annual evaluation report (USAFE, IEAFA, and Air University officials).

Third, there are institutional challenges to developing a robust human-aspects capability within the SC arena. For FAOs and conventional Air Advisors, doing a tour of advising requires spending time outside their primary career fields. However, rather than competing with other individuals doing similar jobs, they must compete for promotion against their peers doing more traditional jobs within their career fields. This leaves them at a disadvantage. Many FAOs we interviewed enjoyed their work greatly, but they felt that their SC tours might negatively affect their career advancement potential. While Air Education and Training Command (AETC) and the Air Advisor Flight are working to make the Air Advisor designator more highly valued within the Air Force, they acknowledge that changing institutional culture will take time. In the meantime, some airmen may avoid SC assignments because of the perception that such assignments can negatively impact their Air Force careers (AETC and Air Advisor School officials).

Finally, we found an interesting nexus between the SC and IO fields whereby they could be mutually supporting. Some SC professionals we engaged noted an unfortunate failure to systematically use IO capabilities in SC planning. As noted, interviewees consider it essential to have human aspects be a core part of the planning process, particularly from the angle of understanding how to best use a spectrum of SC tools to achieve the strategic vision for a particular country or even operation. This would suggest that an IO officer would be an essential part of the A5 plans team (where SC planners often reside) within the component commands. However, in some commands there is no position for IO officer in the A5—they are instead located in the Air Operations Center, which according to USAFE officials "focuses on the greatest threat, instead of all the other phases before and after combat," including SC. This absence, they argue, limits the effectiveness of SC efforts to achieve long-lasting effects (author discussions with USAFE officials, Ramstein Air Base, Germany, May 2018).

In sum, a broad swath of SC professionals in the Air Force works frequently with other nations to build partnerships in pursuit of U.S. national security interests. However, there are shortfalls in training, experience, and career management that create obstacles to understanding human aspects across this mission area. In addition, while the impacts of investing in human-aspects-sensitive SC operations may be challenging to assess, there are methods being developed that the Air Force could more systematically employ to measure the effectiveness of such activities.

Cyberspace

Cyberspace is a relatively new warfighting domain for the United States, and DoD's understanding of how to conceptualize and operate within this complex and evolving domain continues to mature (Welch, 2011). As such, researchers have only recently begun to thoroughly consider the human-centered aspects involved in the cyberspace warfighting domain, including the roles and responsibilities of operators and the human awareness they require to address threats (Vieane et al., 2016). This consideration has, at least in part, stemmed from recognition that human cognition is a key component within the information and cyber environments (Varga, Winkelholz, and Traber-Burden, 2016).

Human Aspects in Cyber Strategy and Operations

To effectively execute operations in cyberspace and address the subsequent effects of these operations, researchers and others have argued that cyber operators should have strategic-level knowledge and understanding of the activities that different agencies within the United States and governments and organizations around the world are conducting in cyberspace (Arwood, 2007; Luiijf, Besseling, and de Graaf, 2013). This may include, for example, a consideration of how government agencies and allies are promoting a culture of cybersecurity by increasing the awareness among different populations of cyberspace threats and working with these entities to share information and coordinate activities (DoD, 2015; Luiijf, Besseling, and de Graaf, 2013). Organizations and governments might customize information to address the ways in which distinct populations understand and use cyber systems, and they can tailor selection and training for individuals who are implementing cyberspace efforts (Bada, Sasse, and Nurse, 2015). As such, knowledge and awareness of cyber culture may provide strategic insights. Building a strategic-level understanding may also consist of a review of other, potentially more nefarious actions, being taken by other groups or governments to influence populations through the use of cyber capabilities, consideration of why these tactics may or may not be effective within and across different populations, and development of strategies to counter these different tactical categories.

Addressing the human aspects of cyber operations, researchers have proposed that cyber interactions between nation-states occur in the context of an extended, multilayered history of interactions between entities, with these layers including military, diplomatic, social, and cultural elements (Valeriano and Maness, 2014). The reasoning is that a broader social context influencing cyber activities can apply not only to nation-states but also to smaller organizations and communities, or nonstate groups, that may also have an online presence (Vaishnav, Choucri, and Clark, 2013). Therefore, by better understanding the history of interactions between groups— including nation-states and nonstate groups, functional norms regarding the impacts of operations on civilians, and potential motivations to expand power and status—cyber operators can better anticipate the cyber methods that different entities may use during incidents, who is most likely to be the targets of these methods, and how those targets might respond.

When they are supporting or conducting operations, cyber operators should have thorough situational awareness (Vieane et al., 2016). This encompasses, but is not limited to, knowledge regarding technical elements and capabilities. It also includes awareness of who is taking what actions, why they are doing these things, how and where they are doing them, the potential impact of the actions, and plausible options for effectively addressing the actions (Barford et al., 2010). For example, knowledge regarding which cyber forums different social or cultural groups frequent and how these groups respond to sociodigital influence efforts can inform the tactics that cyber operators pursue (Knott, 2014). Cyber situation awareness can be improved through an understanding of human aspects, including cognition and motivation, and researchers have described human elements as a common thread across cyber threats, such that hackers exploit the perceptions and motivations of users to address their own intents (Marble et al., 2015).

Human-Aspects-Related Training in Cyber

Although consideration of human aspects is important to successful cyber operations, current training and exercises appear to heavily emphasize technical information and capabilities, with limited consideration of human aspects (Babcock, 2015; Vautrinot, 2012). Interviewees noted the potential utility of providing information on human aspects during classroom training, which is further supported by creating wargames and exercises that fully incorporate cyber operators. These would allow cyber operators to interact with individuals outside the cyber career field, consider strategic-level coordination, and deliberate regarding appropriate tactics to implement, based on notional population characteristics, motivations, and perceptions (cyberspace officials).

Thus, broadly, cyberspace is a constantly developing, man-made construction that is heavily influenced by human cognition and actions. Human thoughts and behaviors are influenced by, for example, historical and current inter- and intra-group interactions, cultural norms and beliefs, and individual knowledge and skills. Therefore, understanding these elements, both broadly and as related to specific populations of interest, may enhance cyber operator capabilities. However, although these are critical human-based aspects of this domain, current training for Air Force cyber operators appears to underemphasize human-related aspects.

Space

Space is considered an increasingly congested and contested environment, requiring international coordination and cooperation to understand and address potential threats, including man-made disturbances from various actors (Lynn, 2011). An understanding of and, when possible and appropriate, alignment with the goals and desires of diverse countries and groups can facilitate successful interactions in this area (White House, 2010). However, understanding and knowing the differences between purely military or military-civilian space-based assets will be important for considering the second- and third-order effects of targeting such assets and knowing how an opponent may use space-based assets. Additionally, data uplinks and downlinks are often terrestrial and therefore require an awareness of the perceptions of local populations. Finally, space assets are primarily a means for conveying information, and like cyber can be part of a multi-domain operation to achieve effects in the information environment (USAF cyber official). Overall, then, there appear to be many human-based considerations for conducting operations in space, supporting these operations from earth, and coordinating space operations.

Human Aspects in Space Strategy and Operations

At a strategic level, an understanding of how other countries and groups perceive the United States, how they conceptualize operations in space, and what sociohistorical factors contribute to these perceptions can help the United States determine the potential for and extent of possible cooperation and coordination in space. Most recently, analyses of the comments and assessments published by Chinese analysts demonstrate how consideration of human dimensions can help to inform potential U.S. space strategies. Different researchers have, for example, commented on historical changes in China's perceptions regarding modern technology and the utility of space capabilities, concerns regarding hegemonism and neointerventionism, and current perceptions regarding the importance of achieving space superiority to prevent potential international threats (Cheng, 2012; Pollpeter, 2016). Analyses regarding perceptions within other countries of the international structure and strengths and weaknesses to coordination in outer space suggest potential considerations and obstacles that the United States can address in its space strategy.

Some evidence suggests that the United States military is aware of and has considered the utility of these analyses. For example, one issue of the Air Force Space Command's discontinued journal for space and cyberspace professionals, *High Frontier*, focused on international coordination in space (Air Force Space Command, 2010). Several articles in this volume addressed language, cultural, and other social issues that can arise when multiple countries, organizations, and industries are engaged in space operations.

Beyond strategy, activities and operations in space may also benefit from consideration of human elements. For example, fear and suspicion among nation-states and private entities may motivate some international activities in space. Some have proposed that, to better understand potential space activities and measures, consideration of terrestrial behaviors and operations is worthwhile (e.g., Robinson, 2016). For example, the past behaviors of different actors and broad social norms exhibited in other domains, such as sea, might provide guidance for how entities will act and respond to actions in space. Nations and groups might respond differently to similar operations, based on the extent to which their military and civilians would be impacted by space activities, and on perceptions regarding who is conducting the activities and why. Similar to cyber, knowledge and understanding regarding behavioral norms, the reliance of populations on space-based technology (e.g., satellites), and previous behaviors of and interactions between nations and groups in other domains—all human-relevant aspects—might inform space operations.

The Air Force has different officer and enlisted career fields that conduct or support space operations (e.g., Enlisted AFSC classification 1C6XX, Officer AFSC classification 13AX, 13SX). Specialty qualifications for these career fields tend to stress technical knowledge and education, but some emphasis is also placed on the utility of understanding the human aspects influencing and involved in space operations—addressing, for example, proficiency in communication (13AX) and knowledge of space history and organizations (13SX).

In terms of the training that those conducting or supporting space operations receive, previous research suggests that this training emphasizes system operations, with limited focus on recognizing and responding to allied and adversary space actions and few exercises involving space operators addressing responses to these actions (McLeod et al., 2016). Recent structural changes to this training demonstrate an increased awareness regarding the importance of communication and coordination with allies. Specifically, by 2019, Air Force space training is to be opened to allied countries, and it will also include a new course addressing space situational awareness (Air Force Public Affairs, 2018). In part, these changes have been put in place to improve communication and cooperative actions in space (Insinna, 2018).

Space-based operations can benefit from an awareness of the effects of these operations on diverse groups; competent communication and coordination with various governments and organizations; and anticipation of future adversarial actions. These are all human-based aspects of space operations. However, generally, the human elements of space operations appear to have been underemphasized in Air Force training and education. Although recent modifications to space training may improve coordination with allied countries, additional information regarding how groups perceive, currently use, and plan to use space-based capabilities may enhance operators' capabilities.

Other Air Force Missions That Engage in Human Aspects of Military Operations

In addition to these major categories of career fields and mission sets, there are a number of other areas where human aspects are essential for success, including elements of base operations, instructing, and the Office of Special Investigations (OSI).

Base operations can encompass a wide variety of responsibilities, including some often run by civilians. When negotiating access to bases or land in foreign countries, base security, logistics and contracting, hospitality services, and the base commander all may have a role that involves interacting with people from foreign cultures, particularly in a deployed environment. For example, we interviewed one person involved in SC who had been sent to negotiate access to use a partner military base. This interlocutor lamented having not had any training in cross-cultural communication or negotiations prior to that engagement, particularly as the negotiation was with a foreign general officer. For more established bases in foreign countries, the base commander, logistics and acquisition personnel, and members of the hospitality and security forces teams may all find themselves interacting with members of the host nation population. According to interviewees, these officers often get basic culture training on arriving to the foreign country that outlines points of etiquette, but no deeper training in cross-cultural skills such as that provided for Air Advisors, despite similar or greater levels of engagement.

Interviewees explained that such preparation is particularly important for base commanders, as they can be asked to participate in local community politics, such as the base commander for Kadena Air Base in Okinawa, who is expected to represent the American forces as a mayor and to sit on a local mayor's council. The Air Force Culture and Language Center (AFCLC) conducted one-off training of this kind for such a commander, but this training was on request and has not yet been institutionalized. Although it is most obviously applicable in a deployed environment, for bases that regularly host foreign nationals, providing similar training for these sorts of personnel would also be of benefit. The Air Advisor Flight has provided such trainings in the past, but again, on a one-off, on-request basis, rather than as a consistent requirement (AFCLC, Air Advisor Flight officials).

According to other interlocutors, cross-cultural competency courses should also be a standard part of instructor training. They suggested that such training would have been incredibly useful for instructors working at education and training institutions who interact with foreign students but emphasized that those same skills are equally relevant to dealing with a diverse student population. They also noted that at the heart of many cross-cultural skills is developing emotional intelligence, which is useful in all instructor contexts (IEAFA officials).

On the other hand, personnel in the OSI are among some of the best prepared to interact with people from other cultures on a tactical level. Building rapport and understanding people's motivations are inherent skill requirements for conducting interviews and operations as Special Agents. According to an OSI representative we interviewed, when operating in another country (or with anyone), "Knowing the basics of how to talk to someone who's different is a necessity. If we are dealing with a group or individual who is not used to interacting with the U.S., then knowing the specifics of the other's culture and language becomes increasingly necessary" (Author discussions with OSI officials, Hulburt Field, Fla., October 2017). As a result, there are specific positions within OSI that have language requirements. Initial training for OSI personnel is designed to provide them with an understanding of people and their motivations; then they learn explicitly how to do this in a cross-cultural environment in predeployment training and in advanced interview training.[4] One OSI interviewee felt that it would be helpful to have more of the cross-cultural aspect in initial skills training, as well as greater training on U.S. cultural values to understand differences in humor and values. This type of training early on would better prepare Special Agents and other personnel who are sent overseas on their first tour and currently are not yet exposed to such training at that point in their career.

---

[4] It was beyond the scope of the current study to evaluate the effectiveness of this training.

In summary, for some of these other Air Force missions that require an understanding of human aspects in military operations, there seems to be adequate training and application in operations, while for others, gaps exist. According to OSI officials, OSI human-aspects training is very positive and does a good job of preparing Special Agents to conduct their incredibly human-centric mission in a wide variety of locations. As such, OSI curricula could serve as a source for other tactical-level human-aspects training across the Air Force. On the other hand, there appear to be gaps elsewhere that have been identified through emerging needs in the field—for example, the need for deep understanding by base commanders and other officials of the societal and cultural norms and traditions among communities "outside the wire." In light of the USAF presence on airbases around the world, base officials may need more systematic education and training prior to assignment.

Broader Institutional Challenges in Incorporating Human Aspects into Air Force Operations

In discussing how and where to incorporate human aspects into Air Force and military operations, we identified several institutional challenges that will make it more difficult to implement in a systematic and holistic way. Overcoming or working around some of these challenges will greatly enable the consistent and systematic use of human considerations in all aspects of planning and operations.

- ***Technology-centric culture:*** Numerous stakeholders emphasized that the Air Force as an institution is very technology focused, seeking out the most advanced machinery and computer-based modeling and simulations to achieve its ends. In such an environment, making a case for the intensive but very analog capabilities that are required for engaging in human aspects of operations is difficult.
- ***Lack of leadership support for incorporating human aspects into planning and conducting military operations:*** From intelligence personnel to IO officers, USAF personnel noted that to effectively incorporate human aspects into planning and operating in air campaigns, leaders and planners have to buy into the concept. Without this support, alternative options or complementary messaging efforts in the planning process will likely be unsuccessful. Currently, support for human aspects of military operations is individualized rather than systematic; as a result, whether or not human aspects are incorporated into operations has become personality dependent.
- ***Lack of depth of expertise:*** Effective use of human aspects at the strategic and operational levels requires both a full incorporation of these elements in the planning process and the specific knowledge about a given culture or society that will fully utilize this capability. Lacking a readily available pool of experts limits the second half of that requirement and thereby potentially reduces the effect of any human-aspects engagement.[5] NASIC has a cell dedicated to providing expertise as a reachback center, but it is limited in size and scope. Further, it can take time to develop the appropriate levels of depth for a

---

[5] This fact is equally true at the tactical level for air advisors and those engaged in SC, but such personnel often receive more specific training to support that need.

particular country or region. For many information officers and other practitioners of human aspects of military operations, this support is necessary but insufficient to meet their needs.

- **_Difficulty in measuring effectiveness:_** Influencing the human environment is a complex and challenging endeavor that often only reflects progress after extended engagements over a long span of time. Moreover, when an impact is made, the result is often that something bad does not happen, and measuring a negative is inherently difficult. Nongovernment agencies and development organizations routinely struggle with the challenge of ensuring that their efforts are achieving the desired ends. Similarly, continued funding for aid programs is often contingent on showing tangible results. In the military context, this challenge is made more poignant by the fact that personnel evaluations and ultimately promotions are based on quantitative factors that are measured during an annual review cycle. Thus, there is not a focus on trying to develop the qualitative and long-term assessments that human aspects demand.

- **_Limited career prospects in some fields requiring high human-aspects understanding:_** SC experts and IO officers (as well as Civil Affairs and Psychological Operations personnel in the Army), and career fields or tours of duty that focus on human aspects are often valued less in Air Force culture than their more kinetic counterparts. For example, we were told that a tour as an air advisor can be detrimental to one's career progression, that FAOs often have a difficult time competing against their peers who are still active in their primary career fields, and that the IO career field currently tops out at the lieutenant colonel rank. As a result, enticing career-minded individuals into these fields can be challenging.

- **_Lack of priority given to support for human aspects of military operations across services:_** Even when it is written in doctrine or guidance to consider human elements in planning, there are no forcing functions to ensure that happens. In closed environments such as wargames or exercises, human aspects are often given only a token role, with conventional kinetic activities taking up the bulk of the time and energy. Similarly, in times of budget cuts, human-aspects capabilities have historically been some of the first ones to lose funding, facing deep reductions to and eliminations of their capacity (e.g., the reduction of the AFCLC by two-thirds of its capacity).

Summary

An important takeaway from this survey of career fields and positions requiring high levels of understanding of human aspects is that there are important pockets of training and integration of human-focused capabilities, but these efforts are not incorporated systematically in a way that would suggest broad understanding and priority across the Air Force. Our exploration indicates that developing airmen with a stronger appreciation of human aspects in operational environments is a worthwhile goal and should be more broadly and systematically applied. In the next chapter, we consider how human aspects are addressed by other U.S. military services and foreign militaries to gain further insight into how to incorporate human aspects into Air Force operations more broadly.

4. Frameworks for Integrating Human-Aspects Considerations from Other U.S. Military Services and Foreign Military Partners

In this chapter, we explore how human aspects in military operations is incorporated into the strategy and planning, operations, and training of the broader U.S. military, both joint operations and within the other individual services, as well as within the militaries of two select international partners, the UK and Germany. We selected the U.S. military services and international partners in consultation with our sponsor in an effort to examine whether there may be models or effective practices of incorporating human aspects of military operations that the Air Force could draw on. Here, we describe our findings and discuss ways in which these models may be relevant to Air Force efforts to improve integrating human aspects into military operations.

Human Aspects in the U.S. Military

Human Aspects in Joint Military Doctrine

Our review of doctrine found that joint doctrine does not formally address human-focused capabilities in an integrated way, but a number of JPs (including those already described in Chapter 2) describe factors that include consideration of the human aspects of military operations. For example, there is a recognition in doctrine that the United States must account for human terrain and a general recognition that the more knowledge U.S. forces have of a society they are engaged with, the better. However, operationally, doctrine focuses on how U.S. forces protect, manage, and influence populations. JP 3-0, *Joint Operations* (2011), lists the types of operations that affect the human terrain. These include stability operations (SASO), and civil affairs, humanitarian assistance, and counterinsurgency (COIN), among others. JP 3-07, *Stability* (2009), directly addresses human aspects by arguing for the necessity of strengthening the legitimacy of a host nation.

These publications also indicate that protection of local populations is a requirement for the U.S. military. For example, the JPs addressing Foreign Internal Defense, SASO, Civil-Military Operations, and COIN each discuss operational methods for U.S. forces to provide security to populations. The primary focus of many of these documents, however, is in the development of partner nation security forces, with little discussion given to how to tie those military developments with sociopolitical factors.

Other documents, such as JP 3-06, *Joint Urban Operations* (2013), take a different approach and discuss the need to manage populations. JP 3-06 talks about the need for U.S. forces to not harm civilians during operations. It additionally recognizes that civilian presence and activities on the battlefield can actively interfere with military operations or hinder effectiveness:

> The Commander should keep in mind the overall objectives regarding the civilian populace: to minimize civilian interference with military operations, minimize mission impact on the population, and observe the necessary legal, moral, and humanitarian obligations towards civilians. (p. II-4)

Moreover, joint U.S. Army-U.S. Marine Corps Field Manual 3-24/Marine Corps Warfighting Publication 3-33.5 (2014) notes that in understanding the operational environment in counterinsurgency,

> culture forms the basis of how people interpret, understand, and respond to events and people around them. Cultural understanding is critical because who a society considers to be legitimate will often be determined by culture and norms. Additionally, counterinsurgency operations will likely be conducted as part of a multinational effort, and understanding the culture of allies and partners is equally critical. (p. 3-1)

Another means of interaction is through Military Information Support Operations (MISO) to influence populations. Influence is doctrinally divided into either increasing or decreasing a population's support for a host nation government. In a conventional combat environment, this entails separating the allegiance of the local population from its government, whereas in unconventional, counterterrorism, or counterinsurgency environments, MISO is intended to increase local support for the host nation government at the direct expense of support for local insurgent or terrorist groups. Each MISO product is the result of a Target Audience Analysis, wherein the MISO team and U.S. commanders consider all sociocultural aspects relevant to understanding how a local population will interpret and respond to a message or operation on behalf of U.S. forces.

Beyond these references for consideration of human aspects in military operations, we found it largely omitted from other aspects of joint doctrine. There is little discussion, for example, of the limits of military operations to affect the human domain. Additionally, we found no explanation as to how military commanders can leverage interagency and civilian organizations. JP 3-22 *Foreign Internal Defense* (2018) is one of the few major joint publications we identified to address how military forces can engage organizations such as the State Department to leverage their capabilities in a campaign, and JP 3-07, *Stability* (2016), discusses stabilization efforts led by the State Department and other non-DoD entities and emphasizes effects on the population of fragile countries. However, there is little guidance about how and when this is needed.

Potential Doctrinal Frameworks for the Air Force

In terms of potential frameworks that could be informative to the Air Force, joint intelligence doctrine offers one possible construct for the types of knowledge that are necessary to integrate human-focused operations. Specifically, *Joint Intelligence Preparation of the Operational Environment* (JP 2-01.3, 2014) and branch-specific field manuals, *Intelligence Preparation of the Battlefield/Battlespace* (ATP 2-01.3/MCRP 2-10B.1, 2014) detail specific information requirements to understand individuals, groups, institutions, and society-specific factors and how they interact with enemy forces. Another document that attempts to provide a deeper exploration of what knowledge is necessary for commanders is JP 3-24, *Counterinsurgency* (2018c). It provides a means of operationalizing understanding of humans for military purposes by instructing commanders to gain an "intimate knowledge of the causes and ongoing grievances of the insurgency" (p. V-1).

The Joint Intelligence Preparation of the Operational Environment (JIPOE) framework for intelligence collection could thus serve as one possible construct to standardize the knowledge necessary for the services to consider human aspects in military operations. JIPOE requirements span intelligence collection requirements ranging from conventional combat to irregular warfare environments. Relevant actors covered by JIPOE requirements range from uncommitted populations to an opposing commander's psychological biases. JIPOE provides a means of capturing socioeconomic information otherwise lost to many commanders, such as population patterns, living conditions, real or perceived historical grievances, national/ethnic/sectarian conflicts and rivalries, languages and dialects, cultural and class distinctions, political attitudes, religious beliefs and laws, education levels, emotional reactions to recent events and changing conditions, information manipulation, and any existing or potential refugee situations.

There are significant drawbacks to using an intelligence framework for knowledge of human aspects that relies solely on classified information. For example, classified intelligence collection is an activity that carries specific legal, policy, operational, and dissemination restrictions. Intelligence, once gathered, can only be disseminated to cleared individuals in designated areas. If collected clandestinely, information regarding social norms, culture, and other necessary information can be too tightly restricted to be disseminated to all personnel with a need to know. Most of these forms of information can often be found in unclassified open sources. Therefore, if human-aspects-related information is relegated to classified intelligence frameworks only, the information may be limited in its usefulness. For this reason, any use of intelligence frameworks must consider the use of open-source intelligence and products that are at least designed for audiences that can receive "For Official Use Only" information and are even releasable to the public.

Thus, while there are some doctrinal references to incorporating human aspects into military operations, consideration of human-focused capabilities appears to be piecemeal. The area that seems doctrinally to emphasize the human element—intelligence—has limitations to broader application. At the same time, careful review of intelligence doctrine might provide the Air Force with a framework for adopting some of the concepts to a doctrine for applying air, space, and cyber power.

Human Aspects in the U.S. Army

Doctrine and Policy

Current Army Operations doctrine (Army Doctrine Publication (ADP) 3.0, *Operations*, 2017) specifically recognizes that war is a human endeavor, stating:

> All war is inherently about changing human behavior, with each side trying to alter the behavior of the other by force of arms. . . . Commanders must continually assess whether their operations are influencing enemies and populations, eroding the enemy's will, and achieving the commanders' intended purpose. (pp. 2–3)

To this end, the Army has recently published several concepts that incorporate the importance of considering human aspects. For example, in 2014, the Army's Training and Doctrine Command (TRADOC) published a functional concept called "Engagement" that focuses heavily on the importance of human aspects in conflict and war and the skills required for engaging with local populations in SC or conventional operations (TRADOC Pam 525-8-5). The Army's functional concept for Movement and Maneuver in 2020-2040 was also recently revised to reflect the importance of human aspects and "recognizes the cognitive aspects of political, human, social, and cultural interactions and the requirement to plan and synchronize engagement efforts to shape security environments, influence key actors, and consolidate gains to achieve operational objectives" (TRADOC Pam 525-3-6, 2017, p. 3). The Army's *Insurgencies and Countering Insurgencies* field manual also places a heavy emphasis on human aspects when discussing the operational environment (FM 3-24, 2014). As additional evidence of the Army's increased focus on human aspects, the Army recently engaged the RAND corporation to conduct a series of research projects focused on better understanding and influencing "will to fight" (see McNerney et al., 2018 and Connable et al., 2018).

The Army's Special Operations community is strongly focused on conceptualizing how they can operationally engage with what they term the "human domain." Their definition of human-domain-related operations, however, focuses on what they call the "gray zone." This represents the population that is neither hostile nor friendly to U.S. military objectives but can be persuaded, through engagement, to partner with U.S. forces.

Army Special Operations Forces (ARSOF) doctrine provides a descriptive layer to operating in the human-focused arena. U.S. Army Special Operations Command (USASOC) in particular has pushed for special operations forces to be considered among the leading actors with expertise on human aspects due to their unique capabilities and their unit alignments according to geographic regions. However, the foremost document describing the operating concept for USASOC regarding human aspects is *USASOC Strategy 2035* (USASOC, 2016). According to the strategy, "ARSOF elements represent a multi-spectrum force, focused on the human terrain, and optimized for competition in the gray zone" (p. 16). The strategy stresses its most robust skill set to be training, advising, and assisting partner forces within the gray zone, whether they are partner nations' counterterrorism forces or insurgent forces. To improve Army special operations capabilities over the next decade, *Strategy 2035* describes a need to invest in language and cultural skills, improve intelligence collection of so-called gray populations, and improve technical capabilities for intelligence sharing.

One area of overlap between the Army's concept of human aspects in military operations and the same concept in joint publications is the emphasis on MISO to influence populations. As Army FM 3-05, *Army Special Operations Forces* (2006), describes, MISO uses Target Audience Analysis to identify the relevant societal factors that can be leveraged in messaging to encourage a target audience to behave more in accordance with U.S. campaign objectives. For operations during the past two decades, this has taken the form of influencing populations to turn against terrorist and insurgent groups such as al Qaeda and the Islamic State. MISO units specifically retain a cadre of civilian cultural SMEs, in-country personnel, and interagency relationships for the cultural and linguistic knowledge necessary to conduct their information support operations.

The U.S. Army also retains several other human-aspects-related capabilities. Its FAO program is the oldest among the U.S. armed services and provides regional expertise to Army commanders. The Army recently stood up the Security Forces Assistance Brigade (SFAB). The SFAB will be regionally aligned by combatant command, enabling them to focus on developing regional expertise and provide security force assistance to partner nations' security forces. This will take the form of advising, assessing, supporting, and liaising with host nation security forces (SFAB, 2018).

Operations

While the conventional Army has incorporated some aspects of human-focused capability in particular mission areas, much of the advanced knowledge and integration of human aspects has—as is the case with its Air Force counterparts—been applied by its special operations community. ARSOF has been engaging in human aspects of military operations since its inception nearly 60 years ago. This engagement with partner populations and armed forces has only increased since 9/11, in both combat and noncombat environments. Traditionally, U.S. Special Forces and other special operations elements have conducted Joint Combined Exchange Training allowing the host nation's armed forces to train with U.S. forces. Since 9/11, however, ARSOF has engaged much more directly with host nation populations and irregular armed actors. In Iraq and Afghanistan, this has included partnering with irregular forces, such as the tribal militias in both countries, training each nation's security forces, and conducting reconstruction and IO campaigns. Meanwhile, Army special operators have deployed continuously throughout North Africa, the Arabian Peninsula, the Philippines, and elsewhere in other roles. In 2016, the 1st Special Forces Command stood up Special Operations Joint Task Force-Operation *Inherent Resolve* to synchronize the fight against the Islamic State throughout the Middle East.

One of the largest human-aspects campaigns ARSOF has helped lead is the Village Stability Operations program in Afghanistan. Special operators utilized their knowledge of tribal politics, economic reconstruction, and institution building to help develop the Afghan Local Police throughout the nation. The Afghan Local Police were modeled on the ancient Afghan tribal security system known as *arbaki* (for background on the *arbaki* system, see Jones and Munoz, 2010). The *arbaki* units are trained and institutionalized under the direction of local tribal *shuras* and overseen by government police commanders. They are meant to supplement other security institutions in Afghanistan such as the Afghan National Army. Building this force required special operations forces to live in rural Afghan communities and understand their local political structures and tribal dynamics.

USASOC faces several near-term challenges when considering human aspects of military operations. One of the most significant challenges for ARSOF since 9/11 has been its size and the worldwide need for ARSOF's capabilities and the high demand for teams in Iraq and Afghanistan. Another issue is the increased complexity of operating environments. Technology, globalization, and mass media have increased opportunities for armed competitors, attention toward U.S. operations, and the number of factors ARSOF must consider when attempting to analyze how best to engage human aspects of military operations.

To overcome these difficulties, *USASOC Strategy 2035* provides for a long-term organizational restructuring plan (USASOC, 2016). The main priority is to provide a full spectrum of capabilities to USASOC and Joint Force commanders for both theaters of combat and competition. 1st U.S. Army Special Forces Command-Airborne was restructured to match the responsibilities of a standard Army Division headquarters tasked with both operational missions and force-provider responsibilities. This command additionally received an organic battalion of military intelligence personnel, and Directorates of Special Warfare and Influence. USASOC is also seeking to better integrate intelligence and information systems technologies to improve the speed and ease with which it can process information at the tactical and operational levels (USASOC, 2016).

Training and Careers

The Army recently stood up an IO career field that, along with intelligence personnel, is directly responsible for consideration of human aspects in military operations. Though they are not official designators, the career field has different branches into which soldiers track to specialize in targeting or sociocultural studies. Army interviewees said that their major challenges are not dissimilar to those faced by the Air Force: a limited career field, little access to specific regional expertise, and limited support from maneuver planners and leaders. The Army representatives we spoke with also noted that in the current Army Command and General Staff College, there is only one mention made of IO in a single slide, which means that officers are not learning about this capability and what it might offer.

In terms of training, USASOC and its John F. Kennedy Special Warfare Center and School remain repositories of many human-aspects-related courses. It conducts language training for all languages that can be related to national security interests. The center houses all Special Forces,

Civil Affairs, and MISO basic and advanced courses. Additionally, there are more specialized courses such as the Special Operations Military Deception Course, Network Development Course, Exploitation Analysis, and Technical Exploitation. Many of these courses are attended by all U.S. military branches, and the teaching cadre associated with them are considered leaders in their fields.

Thus, as with the Air Force, much human-dedicated capability resides in the Army's special operations community. But the Army faces some challenges in considering human aspects that are similar to those in the Air Force. In the conventional Army, there appear to be some shortfalls in the availability of personnel dedicated to human-focused capabilities. However, the Army has a deeper doctrinal pedigree in applying human aspects to conventional military operations, and it emphasizes focused education, experience, and career progression for professionals requiring human-focused capabilities (e.g., FAOs, members of SFABs). The Air Force might look to the Army for insights into broadening its engagement in human aspects in military operations.

Human Aspects in the U.S. Marine Corps

Doctrine and Policy

As the self-described expeditionary force of the United States and the so-called tip of the spear, the Marine Corps perceives itself frequently as the first in contact with foreign populations, and thus considers the human dimension an essential warfighting function (Marine Corps Doctrinal Publication [MCDP] 1-0, 2017. Marine Corps Warfighting Doctrine states:

> because war is a clash between opposing human wills, the human dimension is
> central in war. It is the human dimension which infuses war with its intangible
> moral factors. War is shaped by human nature and is subject to the complexities,
> inconsistencies, and peculiarities which characterize human behavior. (MCDP 1-0,
> 1997)

Marine Corps doctrine is in accordance with JP 1, *Doctrine for the Armed Forces of the United States*, citing Thucydides and Clausewitz that war is an integral part of human nature and a socially sanctioned form of violence to achieve a political purpose (JP 1, 2017). Beyond consideration of the human condition in war, the Marine Corps recognized at least 80 years ago the benefits of understanding a targeted population's psychology, political and cultural beliefs, and values to prevent operational and tactical pitfalls (Headquarters United States Marine Corps, [1940] 1990). By understanding people's cultures and values, Marines recognized that they can more effectively interact, inform, and influence their allies and enemies during times of conflict and peace.

The Marine Corps codified the necessity to understand the human dimension in their MCDP 1-0, *Marine Corps Operations*, under section 3-6, "Planning Considerations." This publication urges commanders to understand factors such as "culture, language, tribal affiliations, and [the] human environment" as a part of the operational environment. As such, the battlespace, or the physical environment in which operations are conducted, considers these cultural and human factors as a key dimension in commanders' thinking regarding "interest, influence, and operations" (MCDP 1-0, 1997). The human dimension is an import factor that Marine commanders must consider before, during, and after the onset of hostilities against a targeted population. In MCDP 1-0, the Marine Corps continually expresses its desire to gain every advantage, including influencing friendly and enemy audiences and utilizing every temporal and psychological advantage possible to improve the commander's decisionmaking process.

Additionally, in recent years, the Marine Corps has published multiple concepts of operation and employment outlining the necessity to dominate the human domain as a means of gaining psychological advantages. For example, the *Marine Corps Operating Concept for Information Operations* (2013) and the 2016 *Marine Corps Operating Concept* emphasize superiority in the information space on the battlefield, because "future conflict will not be dominated by tests of strength that characterize industrial war, it will be dominated by wars fought among the people, where the objective is not to crush an opponent's war making ability but to influence a population's ideas and collective will" (*Marine Corps Operating Concepts*, 2006).

In conjunction with JP 3-13.2, *Military Information Support Operations*, the Marine Corps also issued Marine Corps Order (MCO) 3110.5, *Military Information Support Operations (MISO)*, which states its purpose as "target[ing] foreign audiences to influence their emotions, motives, objective reasoning, and ultimately the behavior of foreign governments, organizations, groups, and individuals in a manner favorable to the originator's objectives" (MCO 3110.5, 2015, p. 1). MISO Marines currently conduct tasks such as psychological operations in which they try to influence or disseminate information, spread disinformation, or disenfranchise terrorist or civilian groups (Snow, 2018). Typically, MISO Marines conducting psychological operations utilize media such as leaflets, radio, or digital methods to influence populations in countries like Iraq and Afghanistan.

Separate from the Marine Corps's ability to influence and target foreign audiences, they are also creating an organic cultural and linguistic program to prepare marines for the battlefields of the future. Importantly, the Marine Corps is receiving its cultural and linguistic guidance from the Joint Chiefs' Language, Regional Expertise, and Culture (LREC) Capability Identification, Planning, and Sourcing instruction (CJCSI, 2013; USMC: LREC, 2016, p. 4). This instruction provides policy guidance to support the DoD Strategic Plan for LREC Capabilities. By developing organic programs, like the Center for Advanced Operational Culture Learning (CAOCL), the Marine Corps can meet the requirements set forth by the Joint Chiefs of Staff, but also tailor its coursework to particular regional hotspots in the future. The Air Force could similarly look to the guidance provided in this policy to bolster its own human-aspects capabilities.

Training and Careers

The Marine Corps's approach to the human domain is predominately split between cultural and linguistic programs and the operationalization of those programs to help shape, inform, and influence targeted populations. The shaping and influencing of foreign audiences is accomplished in several ways, including the use of various military occupational specialties (MOSs) like FAOs, crypto-linguistics, IO personnel, and MISO experts conducting psychological operations (USMC: LREC, 2016). A successful influence operation depends on the Marine Corps's ability to understand an enemy or a targeted population and leverage that information to influence desired groups. As such, the Marine Corps is dedicating more resources to enhance its knowledge of various regions and people around the world.

Prior to Operations Enduring Freedom and Iraqi Freedom, the Marine Corps, and the U.S. military more broadly, did not have cultural training policies that would prepare its members for either theater (Davis, 2010). As such, military commanders wanted to prevent such mistakes in the future and slowly began to invest in a wide variety of cultural and linguistic programs. Currently, the Marine Corps has professional military education (PME) courses and programs to enhance marines' knowledge of a given region to more effectively implement influence operations or IOs. Depending on an enlisted or commissioned marine's rank and MOS, they can enroll in different PME courses or programs. However, during predeployment training, if a marine could not attend specialized culture-oriented training for the region in which they are deploying, the Marine Corps Intelligence Activity (MCIA) will distribute a cultural smart card (similar to the Air Force's Expeditionary Culture Field Guides). In an effort to teach as many marines as possible before a deployment, MCIA's smart card acts as a so-called cheat sheet filled with cultural nuances, expressions, or sayings, and a list of appropriate and inappropriate behaviors in a given region (MCIA, 2010).

LREC programs are now available to all marines online, beginning in Marine Corps Recruiting Depots for enlisted and the Basic School for commissioned officers. As careers progress, the Marine Corps Combat Development Command's regional, culture, and language familiarization (RCLF) program offers service-wide promotion of LREC to sergeants and officers. RCLF represents a concerted effort to increase cultural understanding and linguistic skills as marines are assigned to one of 17 different regions around the world. RCLF builds on the Defense Language Institute's HeadStart 2 program, which offers its participants over 1,000 useful phrases and words in addition to learning about background and history of a region. However, RCLF is a career-long effort that continues to push its participants to learn through cultural exposure and specified courses and programs, depending on the region of study (MARADMIN, 2012).

The CAOCL trains and educates Marines about various regions around the world and helps develop the curriculum for the RCLF program (USMC: LREC, 2016). Similar to RCLF, CAOCL is a career-long training and educational program to enhance marines' LREC capabilities across the service. However, unlike RCLF, CAOCL trains marines to become experts in their field of study and can act as a force multiplier for their assigned duty stations. Commanders value marines of the CAOCL because they further enable their ability to engage, navigate, and inform, and to execute influence operations.

Much like the other services, the Marine Corps is trying to increase its use of cyber, information, and influence operations. A common issue throughout the military, as it relates to fulfilling MOSs in the information and computer space, is recruitment and retention. The Marine Corps is currently trying to expand its existing IO- and MISO-related specialties. The Marine Corps is creating new MOSs, such as 0521 and 1700, and new MISO and cyber operations (Snow, 2018). These types of MOSs are no longer specialty, or secondary, MOSs; instead, they are primary MOSs. As a result, marines who choose to pursue them are more specialized and capable of growing in that field. Additionally, new units, such as the Marine Expeditionary Information Group (MIG) have been actively training and readying new units across the Corps, such as III MIG and I MIG (Snow, 2018).

Thus, unlike the other services, the Marine Corps considers the human dimension an essential warfighting function and has a strong tactical focus on human aspects in military operations. The Marine Corps's desire to further integrate culture and war—human aspects in operations—is not a new idea, and the service's incorporation of the concept in education and training, MOS requirements, and operating concepts continues to evolve. Marine Corps consideration of human aspects is codified in multiple Marine Corps doctrinal publications and actualized through a number of service-wide programs. The emphasis on service-wide activities designed to inculcate marines at all levels with cultural, linguistic, regional, and other types of human-focused knowledge and experience provides an important example of an evolutionary model for the Air Force. In particular, the introduction of human-focused concepts early in the careers of both officers and enlisted personnel is an important observation for the Air Force to consider.

Frameworks for Human Aspects from International Military Partners

Through discussions with military officials in the United Kingdom and Germany, the research team explored the practices of two allied militaries to gain insight into how they view and incorporate human aspects in military operations.

Human Aspects in the British Military

The British military is significantly smaller than the U.S. military, with roughly 140,000 full-time, active-duty personnel across the three forces (Army, Royal Navy/Royal Marines, and the Royal Air Force) (Ministry of Defence, 2017, p. 1). In many respects, British efforts to engage in human aspects of military operations resembles those of the U.S. Army, and units focused on human aspects are largely considered part of maneuver forces, though some also operate in a joint environment at the strategic level. According to representatives from the British military, the terminology used in the UK to refer to the varied concepts that come under the rubric of human aspects includes "information operations," "psychological operations," "human terrain," "human geography," and "human factors," which we shall use here when appropriate. Unless otherwise noted, the information in this section is drawn from interviews with UK defense officials.

Human Aspects in British Doctrine

Much like in the United States, British doctrine exists at the service level and the joint level. At the highest level, human aspects are present in joint doctrine. For instance, in the joint doctrine publication *Campaign Execution* (2012), the word "culture" appears 14 times. The term "joint action" is considered to include fires, maneuver, information activities, and outreach (which includes SC activities), and the publication notes upfront the importance of engaging not just with adversaries but with other actors. The doctrine also emphasizes the importance of full- spectrum targeting:

> Influence is central to all military activity. . . . If influence is the overall outcome, a holistic approach to targeting is required from the outset. This is enabled by a deep understanding of target systems and their critical vulnerabilities. With this understanding planners will be better able to select the most effective and appropriate activity, lethal or non-lethal, to apply. (p. iv)

Human aspects are embedded within all these elements, giving them a high priority from the very beginning. This priority is encapsulated by another joint doctrine publication titled *Understanding and Decision-Making* (2016), which emphasizes the importance of understanding people and the role of human factors in terms of both conducting operations and being an effective leader. Culture and consideration of human aspects also play central roles in the doctrine around planning at the joint level, as derived from North Atlantic Treaty Organization (NATO) guidance on planning (*Allied Joint Doctrine for Operational-Level Planning* [AJP-5], 2013). This joint-level doctrine has been translated by the British Army into a concept known as "integrated action."

> The two central ideas in British Doctrine remain constant. The requirement for Mission Command and the ManoeuvristApproach has not changed, however the latter is focused on the enemy—and in this complex and dynamic environment manoeuvre has to take account of a much broader audience than simply the "enemy." A new idea is therefore required—this is called Integrated Action. It is a unifying doctrine that requires commanders first to identify their outcome; second to study all of the audiences that are relevant to the attainment of the outcome; third to analyse the effects that need to be imparted on the relevant audience; before determining the best mix of capabilities, from soft through to hard power, required to impart effect onto those audiences to achieve the outcome. (*Land Operations*, 2017, p. i)

As with the joint doctrine, understanding the human aspects of military operations is essential to this approach to warfare, from the planning to the execution phases.

Most directly pertinent, however, is a joint doctrine note (which has less weight than a publication) called *Culture and Human Terrain* (2013). This document is akin to the U.S. *Joint Concept for Human Aspects of Military Operations* in that it offers guidance on where and how human aspects should be incorporated in military operations, from strategic- and operational-level planning down to the role of cross-cultural knowledge and skills in tactical interactions.

Human Aspects in British Operations

In order to provide the necessary capabilities that underpin the requirement to incorporate human aspects in plans and operations, the UK has institutions and programs dedicated to this mission. At the joint headquarters level, there are a number of analysis cells with the Defence Intelligence community, including, among others, the Human Factors cell, which "fuses all-source intelligence analysis with psychology, anthropology, human sciences and media expertise to produce valuable and influential assessments [in order to] support operations, diplomatic engagement, policy formation and contingency planning" (see "Psychological Intelligence Analyst," 2016). These analysis cells provide the guidance to commanders and planners on how to incorporate human aspects into strategic and operational planning, as well as the regional and topical expertise to provide the required knowledge of a region or culture. Also at the joint level is the Defence Geographic Centre, which has personnel who specialize in human geography, or the ties between human societies and cultures and terrain, and provide relevant maps to operational units and other government customers (see "A Day in the Life of the UK Defence Geographic Centre," Day of Geography, 2014). The Defence Science and Technology Laboratory is another national-level asset that provides social science and human geography analysis to the military and is exploring the role of machine learning and social media to help better understand the intersection of human populations and military operations (see Dstl, 2018).

In the British Army, there are two major institutions responsible for human aspects at the more tactical level, including the 77th Brigade, which is responsible for the "employment of soft effects," including outreach, psychological operations, defense engagement (the UK's term for SC), and other nonlethal activities that all require understanding and operationalizing human aspects of military operations (Footsoldier, 2015). The personnel at this unit comprise a mix of a small number of active-duty soldiers and a larger proportion of specialized reservists. These reservists are specifically tied to this unit and are selected based on personal or professional backgrounds that are relevant to the unit's mission, such as individuals who work in nongovernmental organizations, social scientists, media and marketing experts, and people with regional experience, among others. This construct can be challenging in that there are limitations on how often and how quickly such reservists can be mobilized to provide input and expertise to projects, but it also allows 77th Brigade to maintain a depth and breadth of mission-specific expertise directly within the military structure rather than relying on contractors or civilians. Such an approach obviates the tensions inherent in having to develop expertise within the military that is equivalent to that received in academia or the professional world while ensuring that such capabilities are organic to the military rather than outsourced and lacking both enduring power and an appropriate understanding of military culture and operations (see Connable, 2018).

The second institution is the Defence Cultural Specialist Unit (DCSU), which serves as a deployable cultural specialist capability. Personnel are trained to different degrees, with some becoming regional experts with language skills and others serving as cultural analysts primarily in a reachback role and so who are less specialized by region. The DCSU was developed to support the missions in Iraq and Afghanistan, but now focuses on other regions of the world and often supports SC efforts, troop deployments, and military exercises. Some of this support comes in the form of providing predeployment culture briefs, but the unit's aim is a deeper use of regional expertise, to provide advice on how to use culture as a lever of influence. The DCSU currently has fewer than 100 people, but they are in high demand, deploying regularly in support of various missions and operations.

Although both the DCSU and 77th Brigade are Army units, they have personnel assigned from all the services, and they provide support to all the services, creating a centralized repository of guidance and expertise on human aspects of military operations.

The British Army has also recently stood up a Specialized Infantry Group, equivalent to the U.S. Army's SFAB, to train and advise partner military forces around the world.

Human Aspects in British Training and Education

The degree to which military personnel receive training on human aspects of military operations varies widely by career field. However, our interviewees noted that there is some element of cultural understanding or human-terrain training that everyone gets at the officer school at Sandhurst or in basic training. As officers proceed through education for command and staffs, they learn about the doctrinal basis for understanding and incorporating nonlethal effects into planning efforts. Intelligence corps training includes cultural intelligence analysis. All these efforts provide some background for developing leaders and personnel who are prepared to incorporate human aspects into planning and operations.

The DCSU requires a high level of training for its personnel, with regional advisors attending extensive language training, language immersion in a host country, a two-week cultural practitioner course on theories of culture and social science, plus additional trainings in various United Nations, NATO, and academic settings. The 77th Brigade and the noted joint-level institutions, however, rely more on the specialized reservists and civilian personnel who are recruited because of their previous expertise, rather than developing those people in-house. Though the DCSU does not provide much training apart from providing culture briefs to units, it has developed a three-day version of its cultural practitioner course that it provides to educate those who might want or need deeper understandings of how to understand and incorporate human-aspects knowledge into operations but do not have a great deal of time to spend in additional training.

The British military does face a number of challenges in incorporating human aspects that are similar to those seen in the U.S. Air Force and other U.S. services, including limited numbers of experts, commanders favoring the kinetic over the nonkinetic, and difficulty in demonstrating effectiveness in a measurable way. However, the 77th Brigade's use of specialized reservists highlights one way the U.S. Air Force might consider ensuring that it has deep expertise that can be brought to bear on a moment's notice. Additionally, the idea of introducing basic human-element concepts early in careers is a recurring theme that might be useful to USAF training institutions.

Human Aspects in the German Military

Germany's military is actively engaged throughout large segments of the world. It maintains at least some presence in Africa, the Middle East, and South Asia as well as engaging on a recurring basis with its European and NATO counterparts. Meanwhile, its training programs have sought to enforce critical thinking among its service members, for both human-rights and military purposes. Unless otherwise noted, information in this section is drawn from interviews with German defense officials.

Human Aspects in German Doctrine

The German Armed Forces, most particularly its Army, the Bundeswehr, and Air Force, the Luftwaffe, fully recognize that human aspects are core to German military operations. As such, there is an emphasis on skill sets related to them. As one of the leaders of NATO, Germany recognizes that it must be able to work with partner nations. Additionally, Germany's history of having its own regionally distinct cultures, dialects, and political priorities has impressed on the nation's leadership that the ability to bridge cultural divides is necessary to any military operation. Germany's participation in the war in Afghanistan further galvanized the need for raising training standards for ethics and cultural understanding. In 2006, photos emerged of a German service member desecrating a human skull found in a mass grave in Afghanistan, angering many and emphasizing the need to institutionalize human aspects across the German military (Cleaver, 2006).

Germany's defense establishment recognizes that it operates its armed services as a member of existing alliances. As a core member of NATO, it prioritizes English- and French-language training for its leadership. All Luftwaffe officers are required to undergo English-language and culture training in their service academy. These same candidates are expected to be capable of giving mission briefings fully in English. Doctrine writers for the German military make significant efforts to ensure that its doctrine is compatible with or matches existing NATO doctrine requirements. There is an understanding that German officers and units must be interoperable with partner NATO militaries as well as other external forces.

Human Aspects in German Operations

Germany retains a small but highly engaged cadre of FAOs. The program is meant to provide the Bundeswehr with cultural expertise and area knowledge. There are just over a dozen FAOs, with near-term plans to develop an accompanying force of noncommissioned officers. The FAO program is also open to civilians, who can apply to fill open positions not filled by military officers. German FAOs have deployed to Iraq in support of Operation Inherent Resolve, Afghanistan, as well as throughout Africa.

Additionally, German officers engage in building partner capacity throughout much of the world. Germany has deployed units to Afghanistan since 2002, playing a key role in building Afghan National Security Forces, including the Afghan Army and Afghan National Police forces. The Bundeswehr's assistance to the Afghan security forces has been ongoing since the fall of the Taliban in late 2001. German Army officers have been embedded since 2014 as trainers in Northern Iraq, assisting the Kurdish Peshmerga forces in the fight against the Islamic State. Additionally, the Luftwaffe and German Navy regularly partner with, assist, and train partner NATO and European forces in response to the growing security threat from Russia.

Human Aspects in German Training and Education

The Bundeswehr has adopted the concept of *Innere Führung*. This concept is directly translated as "inner guidance" but can be considered as critical thinking among service members. *Innere Führung* is meant to assist Germany's military capabilities as well as its geopolitical image. Service members are expected to be cognizant of how their behavior reflects on the German Armed Forces and the nation, and not simply follow orders. This is intended to prevent human rights abuses and alienating local populations, and to enhance decisionmaking capabilities by German service members.

One method of developing *Innere Führung* is an exercise in which service members compare and contrast the differing oaths of service throughout Germany's twentieth century. The oath of service in the Wehrmacht within Hitler's Third Reich is a particular example: Service members pledged their unquestioning loyalty to Hitler himself. Conversely, the current Bundeswehr oath is a pledge to serve the German Republic, its laws, and people.

In German officer training, particularly in the Luftwaffe academy, there is an emphasis on interdisciplinary training and tutoring within the Bundeswehr and other German service branches. Cross-cultural and diversity training, regional studies, ethics, and legal training are all managed by a single office named the Leadership Development and Civic Education Centre, located near Koblenz. The Luftwaffe service academy curriculum stresses the fusion of history, social sciences, and cultural knowledge in order to inform decisionmaking for officers.

While there does not appear to be much in the German military's consideration of human aspects that the U.S. Air Force might incorporate, the country's approach to interdisciplinary training in military educational institutions might provide some insights for U.S. instructors as they develop human-related curricula for U.S. airmen.

Summary

This chapter explored initiatives to incorporate consideration of human aspects in military operations in U.S. service and joint arenas and in selected international military partners. While the Army faces some challenges that are similar to those in the Air Force, it has rooted the human element deeply in doctrine, and it focuses considerable attention on dedicated education, experience, and career management for Army personnel requiring human-focused capabilities—all of which could provide lessons for the Air Force as it seeks to broaden institutional interest in this area. The Marine Corps appears to consider the human dimension even more central to warfighting and codifies it in doctrine while operationalizing it through service-wide programs from time of accession and throughout a career. Finally, the survey of international partners reveals uneven attention to human aspects as well as some insights that the U.S. Air Force might consider, including introducing basic human-element concepts early in careers, careful management of educational requirements throughout careers, and senior leader buy-in into the importance of human-focused capabilities in the service.

With these observations as background, the next chapter explores potential ways in which the U.S. Air Force might broaden appreciation and understanding of human aspects across the force to improve incorporation of the human element in Air Force operations.

5. Deepening Understanding of Human Aspects in Military Operations Within the Air Force

One of the key components of ensuring that human aspects are considered in military planning and operations is ensuring that airmen are educated in their importance and how and when to incorporate these considerations. In this chapter, we describe the current means through which the Air Force provides training and education in this area as well as other methods used for raising awareness of these considerations, such as simulations and wargames. We then identify the gaps and challenges in current human-aspects-related training and education and provide suggestions for better developing these capabilities within the Air Force.

Training and Education

Current Air Force doctrine and force development and education standards reference the importance of training airmen to account for the human aspects of military operations. For example, according to Air Force Doctrine Document (AFDD) 1-1, *Leadership and Force Development* (2011), global, regional, and cultural awareness are listed as core subcompetencies of having an enterprise perspective for Air Force leaders. The 2009 Air Force *Culture, Region and Language Flight Plan* also "envisions cross cultural competency (3C) for all Airmen and robust language skills and regional expertise for targeted Airmen" (United States Air Force, 2009). Further, "global, regional, and cultural awareness" is outlined as a core component to the service's Continuum of Learning that is institutionalized for the development of all airmen (AFPD 36-26, 2015).

In this section, based on our review of training curriculum and interviews with relevant training and education representatives, we outline training and education that the Air Force is conducting that is relevant to developing knowledge and skills related to human aspects of military operations. We also highlight any gaps and challenges in human-aspects-related training and provide recommendations for how to better develop these capabilities within the Air Force. In our review, we are guided by JC-HAMO's principle that the force "must analyze and understand the social, cultural, physical, informational, and psychological elements that influence behavior," (p. 1) and that at least a basic understanding of human aspects among all airmen is required to implement the joint concept. Therefore, we touch on opportunities for developing basic knowledge across the force as well as more focused understanding among certain career fields and positions. To reiterate, human aspects of military operations is a concept the entire USAF needs to embrace because it applies across numerous specialties and activities.

Current Training and Education Related to Human Aspects of Military Operations

Air Force training and education that incorporate consideration of human aspects are extant throughout various training pipelines and career tracks. However, we found that there is no unifying terminology or systemic coordination that ties all human-aspects-related training together, although some of the courses share common attributes and themes.

Initial Training

For both officer and enlisted airmen, training that touches on human aspects in military operations begins at initial training. For example, for officers commissioning into the service through the U.S. Air Force Academy (USAFA), one of the nine defined learning outcomes is that a graduate have an incumbent grasp on the human condition, cultures, and societies. USAFA states that this outcome is important because "[b]eing able to prudently interact with individuals from different milieus resides at the heart of intercultural or cross-cultural competence and includes both domestic and international environments" (USAFA, 2017). Officers commissioning through officer training school also receive some exposure to cross-culture competencies and how they relate to the Air Force mission during their second phase of training (USAF, 2017).[1] However, for officers commissioning through the Air Force Reserve Officer Training Corps, there is no defined module related to human aspects in military operations. Therefore, their exposure to sociocultural knowledge and skills is largely dependent on the types of classes taken as part of their collegiate studies.

For enlisted personnel, all recruits attend basic military training (BMT), which includes lessons involving consideration of human aspects through modules on human relations, antiterrorism/force protection, and joint ethics. In these courses, students are taught about other cultures and about dealing with one's own. According to interviews with BMT curricula designers, the human-relations courses were designed in conjunction with the AFCLC and, in the past, have had sections that specifically focus on relations with people of foreign cultures. That emphasis has largely disappeared in current instruction, but it could be relatively easily reintroduced to help set an initial stage for helping airmen understand human aspects of military operations (AFCLC official).

Following initial training, whether airmen receive additional training related to human aspects in military operations largely depends on the airman's AFSC and the degree to which an airman will interact or deal with foreign cultures. As noted in a previous chapter, the career fields identified as conducting more training that includes human-related aspects are those in IO, SC, intelligence, and OSI career fields. Airmen pursuing an intelligence corps AFSC will, for example, take courses on intercultural competency, critical thinking and analysis, and targeting as part of their skills training. And, although the IO schoolhouse was still in the process of

---

[1] It was beyond the scope of the current project to fully assess the extent and effectiveness of current Air Force training. Instead, our goal was to identify where airmen were receiving at least some exposure to human-aspects-related knowledge and skills.

standing up during the time frame of this research, officers currently in the career field have noted the importance of human-domain-related skills.

Professional Military Education

Throughout their careers, airmen also receive periodic training through PME courses. Officer PME includes courses such as Squadron Officer School (SOS) and intermediate and senior developmental education at Air Command and Staff College and Air War College. In our review, we found that human-aspects-type training is available to airmen at some of these schools, but it is not embedded into the institutional foundation throughout them all. For example, the Regional Culture Studies seminar at the Air War College incorporates an in-depth cultural study followed by immersion in the area of study, but it is not taken until officers are at the lieutenant colonel or colonel level, which is often late to start introducing such ideas. Other courses, such as Culture General courses that teach students about how to understand cultures from a more theoretical level, are currently designated as elective courses for those taking the in-resident Air War College PME, and therefore, they are open only to a small selection of individuals. Similarly, the current SOS curriculum has been shortened, and while human-aspects education used to be a central part of that course, it was one of the blocks that has been removed.[2] At the strategic and operational planning levels, human aspects sometimes are present in courses on multi-domain operations and effects-based planning, but they are not a requirement and so are often not included. Various human-aspects-related courses used to be requirements for all levels of officer PME, but with a loss of capacity in human-aspects expertise (see below), such education is now only minimally available.

For enlisted members, there are elements of human-aspects-related training at the noncommissioned officer academy (NCOA), such as a cross-cultural communications module. However, education and training on human aspects do not consistently build on any foundational structures provided earlier in airmen's careers (USAF instructor). In contrast, teaching related to the Uniform Code of Military Justice (UCMJ), for instance, begins at initial training, and intermediate and advanced UCMJ courses are nested into NCOA and senior noncommissioned officer academy courses. Thus, as an airman reaches a more senior enlisted rank, UCMJ knowledge is very expansive. No such systematic integration of human-aspects-related training is present throughout an enlisted member's career progression.

Additional Education and Training Resources

Outside the traditional training pipelines, two other institutions where training related to human aspects of military operations is available are the Professional Arms Center of Excellence (PACE) and the AFCLC. Although not directly focused on human aspects of military operations, PACE offers a voluntary course on leadership in which many of the skills taught, such as active

---

[2] However, it is still in the curriculum used at the SOS school at the IEAFA (IEAFA instructor).

listening, perspective taking, and dealing with diversity, apply just as much to cross-cultural interactions in the human-aspects sense as they do to leadership of a diverse team. Emphasizing in the course that these skills apply to both realms would be a small way to help develop human-aspects capabilities. The AFCLC "creates and executes language, region and cultural learning programs for Total Force Airmen, and provides the Service with the subject matter expertise required to institutionalize these efforts" (Air University, n.d.). The center executes this mission through a number of programs, including the Language Enabled Airmen Program, regional course work through Air War College, a General Officer Pre-Deployment Acculturation Course, two online courses available to all airmen, an annual symposium, 46 country field guides, and an LREC journal (see Air University, *AFCLC, n.d.*).

Of note among the center's capabilities is the Language Enabled Airmen Program (LEAP). LEAP is a program to help Air Force leadership find airmen with certain language skills to go on temporary duty assignments when a specific language requirement is needed. Those airmen with some language skills already (to exclude linguists in the Air Force) can voluntarily apply to become a LEAP member and, upon selection, are entered into the LEADER program database, a repository of the airmen in the LEAP program that tracks their language skills and experience over time. LEAP participants are also linked with instructors and resources to enhance their language skills (LEAP official).

The AFCLC's staff was cut significantly in recent years, however, and now only seven Ph.D.-level faculty members serve to provide training material and education through each of its program centers (AFCLC official). The center possesses many of the capabilities needed to provide human-aspects and other cross-cultural training and education, but its capacity is unable to meet the demand of the total force alone.

Just-in-Time Training

In addition to defined training through their careers, airmen often receive tactical-level, just-in-time training prior to deployments or when stationed abroad. This training is generally restricted to computer-based training (except for those tasked to be air advisors) and covers basic social etiquette or an overview of local culture provided as an in-brief on arriving in-country. There is little theoretical or foundational background to give airmen a context for human-aspects capabilities or an understanding of sociocultural factors beyond do's and don'ts. While such trainings are popular (interviewees at the AFCLC reported that a high number of airmen view them without a requirement), the depth of learning from these modules is limited (AFCLC official). Finally, AFCLC also offers *Expeditionary Culture Field Guides* for use when deploying abroad. These provide foundational information about culture in general and details about the specific political, social, and cultural milieu of the country. However, they are not part of a consistent education or training effort but serve as an ad hoc resource for those who are interested.

Key Gaps and Challenges in Human-Aspects-Related Training and Education

Coordination

We found that current Air Force education and training regarding human aspects in military operations is incomplete in a number of ways. For example, there appears to be little coordination or systematization of education and training on human aspects. Whether airmen receive an introduction to human aspects and what that entails depends on their AFSC. Officers may receive differing levels of training during their time as cadets; and in PME, they may only be exposed to it as an elective, rather than as a required part of their coursework. For enlisted personnel, educators seek to inculcate junior airmen with critical thinking to help them understand the strategic significance of their actions, but there is no specific focus on developing sociocultural knowledge and skills. Moreover, predeployment training, which does include content on other cultures, is computer-based and can be inconsistent in its depth and breadth and how much is retained.

Unlike the German framework, where there is an office that coordinates all training on cross-cultural skills and knowledge, there is no office that does so in the Air Force. Without any explicit coordination, these training and education opportunities, while useful, are not as consistent and streamlined as they could be if they were explicitly designed to build on one another. AFCLC has been involved in the development of some of the courseware related to human aspects over time, but it does not currently have the resources to ensure that all such training and education are synchronized to be as effective as possible. Making sure that training and education across the Air Force are more coordinated would help to build these capabilities consistently across time and career fields.

Officer Education

Another gap, perhaps a by-product of the fact that there is no overall coordination of human-aspects training, is the lack of consistent emphasis on human aspects in officer education, which contributes to these aspects being largely absent in strategic and operational planning. As numerous interviewees reiterated, it is not enough to have an officer career field dedicated to IO. Commanders and planners must buy in to the usefulness of operating in the human and information environment and the requirements for the kinds of social and cultural knowledge that underpin such an approach. Institutionalized training about not only the importance of understanding the human environment but also how it can and should be used across the full range of Air Force operations will enable the Air Force to be more effective as it focuses on achieving effects rather than just performance.

Having such basic education be consistently present in officer education from the very beginning will help human aspects become part of Air Force culture around planning and decisionmaking. For example, requiring all cadets at the USAFA or in Reserve Officer Training Corps to take at least one social science course would be a way to start building such a sensibility without levying additional demands on the Air Force.[3] If not already required, an introductory course in anthropology, sociology, or social psychology could set a good foundation for consideration of human aspects later in their careers. Building on this background for every officer at SOS, Air Command and Staff College, and Air War College by more explicitly incorporating human aspects into multi-domain planning and operations courses as well as reinvigorating the extant AFCLC-provided courses could help develop this capability in clear and consistent ways that, similarly, do not add an extensive training bill. Interviewees stressed, though, that consistency is key. As one senior officer noted,

> It's too late to teach this at Air War College. Planners and decisionmakers have already learned and applied their ways of thinking by then. It needs to start right at the beginning.

Enlisted Education

Senior enlisted interviewees and educators noted that the consideration of human aspects is just as important on the enlisted side. At AETC, curricula developers said that they felt it was important for even junior airmen to know that what they are doing in operations, regardless of their career field, is all tied into a greater strategic plan that is intended to have a distinct effect. While developing an *Innere Führung* mindset may not be an Air Force cultural goal, the idea that critical thinking is valued and that every action is tied to a plan intended to influence an ally or opponent will help build a foundation for all airmen in considering the human aspects of military operations (German defense officials).

Additionally, at the operational level, some career fields could benefit from increased incorporation of human aspects into their training. As discussed in Chapter 3, these include fields like intelligence, cyber, and space, where there is a need for understanding how the human environment impacts operations as well as for developing or utilizing cultural and linguistic expertise.

Skills for Interacting with Foreign Populations

We also found a gap in developing the tactical skills necessary to enable airmen to effectively operate in and with foreign populations. This challenge, however, is less one of capability than of capacity and reach. Air Advisor training, FAO training, OSI training, and, to some extent, predeployment training are all aimed at developing these skills in different ways and to different levels. Providing this same training to a broader expanse of individuals who might reasonably be expected to interact with host nation populations, such as contracting officers, security forces personnel, and support services, as well as reaching a more complete set of personnel who are involved in SC efforts, would create a significant advantage in preparing these individuals to be

---

[3] This approach is similar to what is done in the French military.

56

more effective. Doing so could leverage some of the training that already exists for those career fields that more regularly provide such training.

Finally, even where there is the knowledge and the will to apply human-aspects considerations to planning and various types of operations, there is often a lack of available resources or expertise on a given region or country. IO officers are employed as generalists, and intelligence personnel often move around enough so that there is not the time or ability to become a functional expert on a given place. Without the expertise to make human-aspects information nuanced, trying to utilize this capability will be far less effective. Institutions like NASIC are limited in size, and not many people know they exist to provide such support.

Similarly, the LEAP program has linguistic expertise, but availability is based on an individual's unit, and participants are largely found rather than developed from scratch. FAOs that develop regional and linguistic expertise are small in number, and due to the dual-track system, they are in non-FAO-type jobs as often as they are available to serve in an FAO capacity. Similarly, MSAS personnel and Air Advisors may develop some degree of regional expertise, but that knowledge is lost once their tour is over. There is no easily obvious solution to this challenge, though some suggestions that were raised include developing an enlisted career field to work alongside IO officers that would be more regionally aligned, ensuring intelligence personnel could specialize in a particular region, employing civilians with expertise, or recruiting or retaining specialized reservists with such expertise, as in the British construct (Air Advisor School, MSAS, AFCLC, and UK defense officials).

Alternative Training Options or Frameworks to Better Develop Human-Aspects-Related Capabilities Within the Air Force

Recommendations to increase training or education often come with a sizable bill to develop new courseware, as well as a time cost for the personnel who must take those courses in addition to the extensive amounts of training and education already required of them. To avoid the latter to the extent possible, our recommendations focus on how such development opportunities could be incorporated into preexisting training requirements—leveraging training and education that already exist in the Air Force or across the U.S. government and that need an enhancement in capacity to provide more broadly.

The Air Force could draw on a number of options and models to help develop capabilities for considering human aspects in military operations. These include drawing from and building on current Air Force training courses already focused on human aspects of military operations, as well as taking advantage of joint- and sister-service courses available throughout DoD. For example, Air Force personnel indicated in interviews that airmen should receive a foundation of human-aspects education early in their careers, which would be built on in PME courses as they progress in their career and rank. Basic human-aspects training could officially and systematically be incorporated into human relations at BMT and in seminars or training blocks across the officer-commissioning sources. Then, that training and education can be built on at NCOA and SOS or other PME courses further along in airmen's careers, including in the Profession of Arms Center of Excellence's leadership development course.

One potential framework is the cross-cultural communications block of study built into the SOS and NCOA curriculum. Instructors at the IEAFA SOS and NCOA course devote a 2.5-hour block during one of the days of study to cross-cultural communication and learning why someone behaves a certain way. Training and education conducted at IEAFA is inherently structured on cross-cultural communication as well. Personnel attending its courses come from 30 NATO armed forces. Instructors at IEAFA noted that USAF personnel, particularly those in SC or other internationally focused careers, acquire a unique skill set from attending SOS or NCOA due to its dense cross-cultural environment.

The Joint Special Operations University (JSOU) also has a number of courses related to the human aspects in military operations that could help to expand Air Force capability. Key courses identified by SMEs include cultural analysis in special operations interagency collaboration, regional studies, and the precommand (USASOC officials; also see JSOU, 2018). The seats billeted in these courses are limited both in number and in the personnel who may attend, but they can be utilized by AFSOC personnel focusing on human aspects of military operations.

Courses at the JSOU and at IEAFA are two examples where training toward human aspects already exists. While the number of seats available to Air Force personnel at JSOU or IEAFA may be limited, utilizing these courses to their full potential and perhaps incorporating the curriculum elsewhere may be more feasible than building curricula and schoolhouses from scratch. In these cases, the Air Force and DoD have a training capability that can be expanded on to reach a broader audience.

The German Armed Forces Leadership Development and Civic Education Center develops unconventional teaching methods that tie together unit cohesion, comradery, and human-aspects-related training. The center has a train-the-trainer program for unit leaders to then present team-building exercises on military ethics, cross-cultural communication, conflict management, and diversity. Three to five hours can be spent on the presentation and, to date, 72,000 hours of such trainings have been distributed throughout the Bundeswehr (German defense officials).

Another inventive method the center has created for the Bundeswehr is the Ethixx board game. The objective of the game is to advance from private to general while progressing across the board. Players are faced with various ethical and moral dilemmas (such as what to do when faced with an armed citizen at a checkpoint) and must make proper decisions in order to advance (such as fire on the armed citizen or seek to arrest them). The game has become a very popular teaching tool that has also helped to strengthen unit cohesion (German defense officials). A similar approach could fit well with AETC's attempts to "game-ify" training and to move training out of the schoolhouse (AETC official). A cross-cultural game that either physically resides at a unit or is available online could help to develop capabilities without requiring specific training time or active trainers.

Our reviews of the literature and interviews with key stakeholders indicate the importance of understanding the human aspects of military operations from the strategic down to the tactical level, and that training on the human aspects of military operations is relevant to all military personnel at the most basic level, but it is particularly critical for those personnel who work most closely in the human domain. Training in human aspects of military operations is provided in some modules of airmen's training throughout their careers. However, like the British 77th Brigade motto, it needs to be baked in, not sprinkled on. Current training exists in bits and pieces throughout the Air Force, but there is currently no systemic and coordinated focus ensuring that appropriate levels of knowledge and skills related to human aspects are included in training and education more broadly across the Air Force.

Modeling and Simulation

Two other means of broadening recognition of the importance of the human dimension throughout the Air Force are modeling and simulation (M&S) and wargaming. The Department of Defense relies heavily on M&S tools and spends about $9 billion annually on their development (Page, 2016). Despite this level of guidance and support, there is no direct mandate to consider or ignore specific topical areas like human aspects in military operations. Therefore, the extent to which M&S tools deal with human domain is largely left up to the services and their individual M&S communities.[4] The Air Force does use some tools that incorporate human aspects, some of which were developed by Air Force organizations. Expanding the use of these tools would be a way to raise awareness and understanding of human aspects in military operations while also refining the tools themselves.

Several tools may be considered as examples. The Athena simulation from NASA's Jet Propulsion Laboratory allows a gamer "to model the political, social-cultural and economic elements of the operational environment and project those dynamics forward in time" and "enables senior leaders . . . to better understand the intended and unintended consequences of a proposed course of action" (Joint Information Operations Warfare Center [JIOWC], 2016). Similarly, the Simulation of Cultural Identities for Prediction of Reactions (SCIPR) model, developed by Aptima, "is designed to help military planners answer the question: 'How will a particular course of action (COA) or sequence of events affect the attitudes or actions of a particular population?'" (Grier et al., 2008). The Air Force Research Laboratory (AFRL) has been involved in developing the National Operational Environment Model (NOEM), which "forecasts regional/national instability," as well as how a Red population would react to a Blue action, and seeks to simulate "the social and behavioral aspects of a populace within their

---

[4] Department of Defense Directive (DoDD) 5000.59 states, "It is DoD policy that M&S is a key enabler of DoD activities" (2007). Department of Defense Instruction (DoDI) 5000.70 created the Defence Modeling and Simulation Coordination Office, which serves as an M&S hub for the services and between the DoD and the rest of the government.

environment, primarily the formation of various interest groups, their believers, their requirements, their grievances, their affinities, and the likelihood of a wide range of their actions" (Maybury, 2011; Salerno, Romano, and Geiler, 2011). There are a number of other Air Force–developed tactical models that could incorporate human aspects if provided resources to pursue development.

An endemic challenge with incorporating human aspects in models and simulations and employing them is that the Air Force, being a technology-focused service, seems predisposed to using these tools for combat or kinetic simulations rather than seeing how they could be used to model operational effects on populations. Analysis of Air Force M&S efforts suggests an emphasis on technological concepts and engineering and physics (Bestard, 2016; AFRL Information Directorate, 2018). Lack of use of human-related tools is not limited to the Air Force, however, and is pervasive throughout the DoD. As one Defense Science Board report asserts, "There is a major shortfall in the availability and maturity of modeling and simulation capabilities that support the planning, rehearsal, execution, and evaluation of population-centric operations. . . . The biggest gaps exist in the analysis tools that would support plan development for Phase 0 operations" (Defense Science Board Task Force, 2011). An in-depth 2018 RAND Arroyo Center study on "will to fight" corroborated the shortfall in addressing human aspects of military operations in military models and simulations, noting, "If will to fight is one of the most important factors in war, and if it is absent or poorly represented in military gaming and simulation, then there is a dangerous gap in existing military games and simulations" (Connable et al., 2018, p. 156).[5] The U.S. Army identified lack of human behavior as a major simulations gap in February 2018 (communication with one of the technical reviewers of this report).

Incorporation and employment of human aspects in M&S tools could become more widespread in the Air Force if there is already a foundation for these considerations in training and education and in strategic planning and operations more broadly. If senior leaders are able to consistently communicate the importance of human-aspects considerations in military operations for the Air Force, it could also help create the connective tissue between disparate sectors within the Air Force, and within the DoD as a whole, that have worked to model culture and human aspects. This would encourage cross collaboration, a broader understanding of the M&S tools that already exist, and appreciation of the importance of including human aspects in these tools. Said one person interviewed, "[T]here are places in the Air Force that model culture—but getting corporate Air Force aware of it is a function of who you know" (Author discussions with AFRL officials, Hurlburt Field, Fla., October 2017). Further development and broader use of such tools should themselves help propagate the importance of considering human-domain concepts throughout the Air Force. Moreover, as these tools are used for training and decision support, lessons will emerge that can form the basis for refining the tools themselves.

---

[5] See Chapter 3 for a detailed review of military models and games, and for experimentation with "will-to-fight" behavioral modifications of existing military models.

Wargaming

There is no single definition of what constitutes a wargame, and little if any official guidance on how to construct one or use its findings. Despite the lack of official doctrine to define and guide wargaming, an increase in senior leader engagement in, and thereby blessing of, wargaming as a valuable tool has sparked a gaming renaissance and triggered an increase in DoD investment of time, money, and energy into both constructing games and understanding how to use them as tools. A 2014 Secretary of Defense memorandum heralded a "reinvigorated wargaming effort" in the department (Hagel, 2014). Despite this resurgence of wargaming, however, there has been no consistent, structured injection of human-focused concepts into wargaming. As a counterpoint, one practitioner noted that "the human domain is the purpose of wargaming. If the human domain isn't in it, it's either a model or a simulation—and a very technical model and simulation at that" (Author discussion with National Defense University [NDU] official, Hurlburt Field, Fla., October 2017). In the Air Force, wargames run out of Air Force Materiel Command (AFMC), AFRL, the LeMay Center, and other organizations deal with the human aspects of war on an inconsistent basis. Wargames in the Air Force tend to focus on testing the technologies and kinetic effects of new capabilities at the strategic and operational levels. For example, wargames conducted by Air University's LeMay Center for Doctrine Development and Education—such as the Joint Land, Aerospace, and Sea Strategic Exercise—are used to determine and analyze responses to crises (Air University, 2017). The USAF's Title 10 wargames, including Unified Engagement and Futures Games, which are run out of the Air Staff, are designed to develop and test concepts of operation against near- and far-term threats.

The 2014 memo from the Secretary of Defense sparked an increase in the use of wargaming as a prognosticative tool, which, problematically, reinforced its narrow scope—especially in the larger showcase games the Air Force runs, such as its Title 10 games. Said one wargamer at RAND, "The Air Force is focused on capabilities during its Title 10 games. Escalation games might be the only area in which it could consider the human domain as important because they are forced to think about the enemy's thought process" (RAND researcher). This reflects the most challenging problem, which is that those who order and participate in wargames have typically not been trained to value human-element-related concepts and so therefore do not think to include them in the games. As one gamer said, "Senior people in the Air Force come out of the flying community. They aren't trained to think about the human domain—they're trained to be pilots." Said an NDU official, "There does seem to be a tyranny of targeting lists. If your ability is strike, then the goal is strike." In other words, the degree to which the Air Force considers human aspects in its wargames is linked to the background of the games' audience and participants. And yet, the importance of understanding the human domain and how it bears out in war is quickly becoming an operational imperative. Said one NDU official involved in the gaming, "As targets become more numerous, it becomes more important to get into the enemy's OODA [observe, orient, decide, act] loop—because we can't get them all. This makes understanding the human domain all that more important" (Author discussions with AFSOC officials, Hurlburt Field, Fla., October 2017). It follows that wargames designed to test the application of weapon systems and concepts on achievement of operational outcomes should incorporate not just physical effects, but effects on target populations as well that might help determine those outcomes.

There are a few possible ways to more fully integrate the human aspects of warfare into wargames. One solution would be to construct games that obviously show the impact that misunderstanding the human dimension can have on an operational outcome. Gamers at NDU suggested that creating a game to run through "a scenario in which the relevant effects that one is trying to generate are not explicitly physical, that you're not denying a capability" would get around the tendency among Air Force gamers to say, "If we knew more about X, we might get better results." To practitioners, this is emblematic of what can often be the approach the Air Force takes, described as a "get that thing" problem (author discussion with NDU official, Honolulu, H.I., June 2018). Breaking the mental stovepiping that can inhibit creative thinking, during both game construction and game play, would help players make the connection between human-focused concepts and operational impact.

A second option would be to use those models and simulations that examine human elements to help create the wargame's scenario. At the beginning of the processes, a simulation might run an array of possible or expected behaviors to bound the possible outcomes of the scenario. During the game itself, how the Blue and Red teams behave becomes an additional factor that can be measured against what the simulation suggested might happen. Where there is deviance, this can help both refine the simulation and suggest alternative approaches both teams might consider (Johns Hopkins Advanced Propulsion Laboratory researcher).

Of course, incorporating the human dimension more systematically in Air Force education and training would itself become a forcing function for designers of wargames. Broader understanding of these concepts would help ensure that future leaders, gamers, and players demand inclusion of human aspects in wargames and in the exploration of new concepts of operation.

Summary

Although there is widespread acknowledgment of the importance of human-aspects-related knowledge and skills in formal force development and education standards and some common attributes and themes across training programs and games, there is no unifying terminology that ties together all training related to human aspects. Further, there is little coordination or systematization of education and training on human aspects in military operations. Without any explicit coordination, these training and education opportunities are not as effective as they could be if they were explicitly designed to build on one another. Building a more systematic and coordinated effort related to officer and enlisted PME can help ensure that considerations of human aspects become part of Air Force culture around planning and decisionmaking. At the operational level, we also found that some career fields could benefit from increased incorporation of human aspects into their training (e.g., intelligence, cyber, and space).

In addition to more formal training and education, awareness of the importance of human aspects in military operations can also be developed through the models and simulations the Air Force uses, as well as in some of the wargames the Air Force conducts. However, in both cases, we found that such concepts are incorporated in a more ad hoc rather than coordinated manner. There are senior leaders in the Air Force's science and technology community who believe in the value of the human domain, however, and their leadership in identifying and synchronizing relevant tools could help spread human-domain concepts throughout the community.

Spreading such concepts into the wargaming space might prove to be more complicated. The Air Force, owing to its technological bent, has a capability- and platform-focused view of warfare. Air Force leadership, therefore, has arguably come to rely on wargaming to perform a limited task—namely, to find out how new capabilities and operational and tactical concepts affect the mathematical results of a conflict. Broadening the aperture of wargaming to include human-domain concepts might rely on a more profound evolution within the culture of the Air Force itself, one that would need to change how airmen are educated and trained for the wars the Air Force will fight in the future. If the Air Force doesn't consider it important to understand the human aspects of war, then it will not train its airmen to consider them, and neither will it run a wargame that includes them.

6. Conclusion and Recommendations

Though there is a focus in the Air Force on integrating all available capabilities into multi-domain operations, there is often a lack of attention paid toward human aspects of military operations compared to leveraging new technological aspects of warfare. However, understanding the social, cultural, physical, informational, and psychological elements that determine our partner nations' and the adversary's motivations, thinking, influence, activities, and recruitment is critical to ensure fully effective application of air, space, and cyber power.

In this report, we assessed whether there is a precedent and need for a new warfighting domain focused on consideration of these human aspects. Although there is strong support for the importance of human-aspects-related capabilities, we found fairly widespread hesitation about the theoretical need for a distinct human warfighting domain among the SMEs and stakeholders we interviewed, and we identified pragmatic constraints on resources that would make developing a new domain challenging. Therefore, we conclude that developing a formal human domain at this time is not likely or necessarily advantageous.

However, with the development and publication of the JC-HAMO, the Air Force is at a unique moment where it will have an opportunity to articulate the human-aspects needs of the Air Force, develop them into Air Force doctrine, and determine where and how to spend resources on developing the needed capabilities. In this report, we identify potential gaps in the current state of Air Force efforts related to human aspects of military operations, including relevant doctrine and training and education. Based on our findings, we provided recommendations throughout the report regarding how sociocultural knowledge and capabilities related to this concept could systematically be integrated into conventional Air Force multi-domain operations. We now summarize those recommendations below under three overarching themes.

Institutional Recommendations

Though we found evidence that human aspects of military operations were considered to some degree in Air Force doctrine and activities, we found that the concept is not systematically institutionalized in the conventional Air Force and that existing capabilities related to human aspects of military operations failed to meet needed capabilities in several mission areas. Based on these findings, we provide several institutional-level recommendations that would allow the Air Force to more effectively integrate human-aspects considerations into multi-domain operations. These recommendations are as follows:

- ***Develop USAF guidance that reflects the JC-HAMO.*** Human aspects are an essential part of modern Air Force operations. From the strategic to the tactical level, understanding adversaries, allies, and populations and being able to operationalize that understanding across the full spectrum of Air Force activities will be a vital set of capabilities going forward. We therefore recommend that the Air Force leverage the JC-HAMO to develop the Air Force's own internal guidance about who should be knowledgeable in human aspects of military operations and how that information should be used to ensure it is consistently and systematically applied.

- **_Better integrate human-aspects considerations into Air Force strategic planning and operation._**
  - _Highlight human aspects of military operations in senior-leader communications to ensure that Air Force culture values not only high technology but also the effects that the application of airpower can have on target populations._ The world of today is already seeing a close alignment of people and technology, from airframes to cyber and space assets. However, in military engagement, the true targets are the audiences of decisionmakers who are influenced by those tools. Decisions about operations should always focus on achieving those effects by the most efficient methods available. These methods may not always be high-tech options but may involve multiple methods of influence to secure vital U.S. interests.
  - _Better incorporate consideration of human aspects into wargames and exercises._ For senior leaders and planners, wargames and exercises provide a unique opportunity to utilize the full range of tools available for warfighting. Consideration of human aspects are often sidelined in such sessions, however. More explicitly incorporating human aspects in both kinetic and nonkinetic scenarios will help to determine where and how human aspects are important for mission success. This integration of human aspects into wargames also provides another avenue to help fully institutionalize these considerations as part of Air Force culture.

- **_Cultivate SC skills within the Air Force._** SC positions are essential to the Air Force and are critical to ensuring that the Air Force maintains the tactical capability to engage in the human aspects of military operations. However, because being an air advisor and even an FAO to an extent can have a negative impact on a career, the Air Force is stigmatizing rather than cultivating these capabilities. Air Force senior leaders must communicate the importance they see in SC skills and ensure that these positions are viewed as a positive mark on an airman's record during promotion considerations.

- **_Develop an assessment plan._**
  - _Incorporate qualitative and longitudinal evaluation means into mission assessments._ The Air Force, like other services, is often focused on understanding the effectiveness of actions and operations in discrete, quantitative ways. The human environment does not easily lend itself to this sort of analysis, yet it can be detrimental to missions and to careers when success is not so readily measured. We recommend incorporating qualitative and more longitudinal assessment and evaluation means as much as possible to reflect their impacts on mission success. For example, social media can identify short-term patterns in attitudes of local populations. If used for longer-term trend analysis with a solid baseline, the right language, and knowledge of locally popular social media, such analysis may help to provide a means of evaluating effect.
  - _Build in assessment of the target audience from the beginning of any plan._ Kinetic and nonkinetic operations can both have long-term human-aspects impacts. Building in means for assessing these missions during the planning phase will help ensure that over the long run, the Air Force has the intended effects with any and all operations.

Training and Education Recommendations

A key component of institutionalizing the importance of human-aspects considerations in multi-domain operations is ensuring that airmen are provided exposure to these concepts early on, and that the training is reinforced or expanded on as needed as they progress in their careers. Based on our review of current training and education in the Air Force, we found that although there is some acknowledgment of the importance of human-aspects-related knowledge and skills in certain places, there is no unifying terminology, and there is a lack of coordination or systematization of education and training. At the operational level, we also found gaps between the demand for these capabilities and the availability of education and training for airmen in relevant career fields (e.g., intelligence, cyber, and space). Based on these study findings, we identified several training-and-education-related recommendations for improving knowledge and skills related to human aspects in military operations.

- ***Give airmen (officers and enlisted) an early introduction to human aspects in military operations.*** Within BMT for enlisted airmen and through the various officer-commissioning sources, ensure that requirements include exposure to the social sciences and the role of human aspects in military operations to provide a foundation on which further PME could build. For example, the Air Force could perhaps make it a requirement for all cadets at the USAFA and in the Reserve Officer Training Corps to take at least one social science course as an elective, at a minimum, which is consistent with a framework used by the French. Doing so would provide a foundation on which further PME could build. Similarly, BMT currently features courses on human relations designed to help teach trainees about perspective taking and working with diversity. This class could easily be expanded to mention that the same principles apply when dealing with foreign cultures as allies or opponents. Like the German *Innere Führung*, it may also be worth reinforcing to all airmen the importance of human aspects to the strategic mission of the Air Force.
- ***Institutionalize required human-aspects curricula in all levels of air education and training.*** Human aspects of military operations need to be a part of the required curricula of education and training programs throughout the Air Force. Such education is critical for developing planners and senior leaders who consistently consider and value sociocultural knowledge and capabilities. Education on human aspects of military operations should be reiterated and developed throughout an airman's PME and considered by officers and noncommissioned officers on both the operational and strategic level. This does not mean that every airman needs be an expert in the human aspects of military operations, but that every airman be at least exposed to these concepts. Experts can and should be leveraged as needed.
- ***Identify a centralized institution to take responsibility for human-aspects education coordination.*** Curricula on human aspects is most effective if it builds on previous education and training. Ensuring that there is one centralized office that is responsible for coordinating this courseware will help ensure consistency and reduce ad hoc training. The AFCLC or perhaps the IO technical training schoolhouse are two potential options.
- ***Better incorporate nonkinetic effects into education for planners.*** Air planners have a tendency to focus on kinetic effects as the primary solution for many military problem

sets. The planning process can be assisted by emphasizing early on that nonkinetic effects working instead of (or, more likely, in tandem with) kinetic effects will likely produce the most effective, efficient outcomes.

- ***Institutionalize cross-cultural skills training for a wider variety of personnel.*** Tactical cross-cultural skills training provided to air advisors would benefit a great many more airmen than currently have access to these courses. All deploying forces, overseas base commanders, people involved in overseas acquisitions, security forces, hospitality, and instructors could benefit from having access to these courses and training in these critical skills.

Recommendations for Developing Regional Human-Aspects Expertise

As a final component to improving the integration of human-aspects considerations into multi-domain operations, our study also pointed to several areas in which more specific regional human-aspects expertise could be developed and utilized. Specifically, we recommend that the Air Force better resource and utilize Air Force–specific reachback capabilities. The lack of readily available expertise on regions and countries within the IO and intelligence career fields limits the effectiveness of planning and operating with human aspects. Having better reachback capabilities within the Air Force will help to prioritize these needs. Organizations such as the NASIC may be well placed to alleviate those challenges. We identified several options for helping further develop the required regional expertise on human aspects within the Air Force.

- ***Consider developing a special experience identifier for regional expertise at the enlisted level.*** Having enlisted airmen identified as having relevant regional experience may allow for the development of regional expertise, which could then be leveraged for use in multiple mission areas.
- ***Consider aligning IO officers and enlisted personnel by geographic region.*** Coding and regionally aligning IO personnel, similar to how Army Civil Affairs and Psychological Operations personnel have been in the past, could allow them to develop methodological and regional expertise and be used more effectively in mission planning and execution.
- ***Consider developing a specialized reservist capability.*** One possible model is the British construct of specialized reservists who are selectively recruited based on specific thematic or regional expertise, and who would be assigned to a single unit and could support a wide range of missions as a reachback capability during their time on duty. Using reservists rather than civilians or contractors brings military perspective into the relevant processes and allows for them to be deployable if needed.

Concluding Thoughts

Human aspects are an inherent element of warfare, and understanding how and where to best influence them is a potentially strong force multiplier across a wide range of operations. In signing off on the JC-HAMO and developing the capabilities and understanding it encompasses from the strategic to the tactical level, the Air Force can begin to pave the way to an ever more effective force that is focused not merely on bombs dropped but also on missions accomplished.

Appendix A. Interview Methods and Participants

Literature Review

As mentioned in Chapter 1, the project team conducted a wide-ranging review of literature on the human domain, other warfighting domains, and related concepts. Policy and doctrine documents were a key component of this literature. The strategic- and operational-level policy and doctrine documents we reviewed are as follows:

- Air Force Annex 3-0, *Operations and Planning*, 2016
- Air Force, *Basic Doctrine*, Volume I, 2015
- Air Force Doctrine Document 1-1, *Leadership and Force Development*, 2011
- Air Force Doctrine Document 2-0, *Global Integrated Intelligence, Surveillance, and Reconnaissance Operations*, 2012
- Air Force Instruction 36-4001, *Air Force Language, Regional Expertise and Culture Program*, 2014
- Air Force Policy Directive 36-26, *Total Force Development and Management*, 2015
- Air Force Policy Directive 36-40, *Air Force Language, Regional Expertise, and Culture Program*, 2018
- *Allied Joint Doctrine for Operational-Level Planning* (AJP-5), NATO, 2013
- Annex 2-0, *Global Integrated ISR Operations*, 2015
- Annex 3-2, Irregular Warfare, *Air Force Capabilities and IW Execution*, 2016
- *Campaign Execution*, Joint Doctrine Publication 3-00, 3rd ed. (UK), 2012
- Chairman of the Joint Chiefs of Staff Instruction, *Language, Regional Expertise, and Culture (LREC) Capability Identification, Planning, and Sourcing*, 2013
- *Culture and Human Terrain*, Joint Doctrine Note 4/13 (UK), 2013
- Department of Defense, *The Department of Defense Cyber Strategy*, 2015
- Department of Defense, *Strategy for Operations in the Information Environment*, 2016
- Department of Defense, *Summary of the 2018 National Defense Strategy of the United States of America*, 2018
- Department of Defense Directive 5000.59, *DoD Modeling and Simulation (M&S) Management*, 2007
- Department of the Army, *Insurgencies and Countering Insurgencies*, FM 3-24/ MCWP 3-33.5, 2014
- Headquarters United States Marine Corps, *Small Wars Manual*, [1940] 1990
- Headquarters United States Marine Corps, *Warfighting*, 1997
- Joint Chiefs of Staff, *Counterinsurgency*, JP 3-24, 2018c
- Joint Chiefs of Staff, *Doctrine for the Armed Forces of the United States, Incorporating Change 1*, JP 1, 2017
- Joint Chiefs of Staff, *Joint Concept for Integrated Campaigning*, 2018a
- Joint Chiefs of Staff, *Joint Concept for Human Aspects of Military Operations (JC-HAMO)*, 2016

- Joint Chiefs of Staff, *Joint Intelligence*, JP 2-0, 2013
- Joint Chiefs of Staff, *Joint Intelligence Preparation of the Operational Environment*, JP 2-01.3, 2014
- Joint Chiefs of Staff, *Joint Operation Planning*, JP 5-0, 2011
- Joint Chiefs of Staff, *Joint Operations*, JP 3-0, 2011
- Joint Chiefs of Staff, *Joint Urban Operations*, JP 3-06, 2013
- Joint Chiefs of Staff, *Military Information Support Operations, Incorporating Change 1*, JP 3-13.2, (2011)
- Joint Chiefs of Staff, *Stability*, JP 3-07, 2016
- Joint Staff Joint Force Development (J7), *Cross-Domain Synergy in Joint Operations: Planner's Guide*, 2016
- *Land Operations*, Army Doctrine Publication AC 71940 (UK), 2017
- White House, *National Space Policy of the United States of America*, 2010
- TRADOC, *U.S. Army Capstone Concept*, PAM 525-3-0, 2012
- TRADOC, *U.S. Army Functional Concept for Movement and Maneuver 2020–2040*, PAM 525-3-6, 2017
- TRADOC, *U.S. Army Functional Concept for Engagement*, Pam 525-8-5, 2014
- United States Air Force, *Air Force Culture, Region and Language Flight Plan*, 2009
- United States Army Special Operations Command, *USASOC Strategy 2035*, 2016
- United States Marine Corps, *Military Information Support Operations (MISO)*, MCO 3110.5, 2015
- United States Special Operations Command, *Operating in the Human Domain*, 2015

Interview Methods and Participants

In addition to reviewing literature and published policy and doctrine, a key data source for this study was semistructured interviews or discussions with relevant SMEs and stakeholders. The goal of these interviews was to better understand perspectives related to the concept of the human domain as well as how consideration of human aspects of military operations is integrated, if at all, into current strategic planning, operations, and training within the Air Force, broader U.S. military, and international military partner efforts. These interviews were held between November 2017 and July 2018, with a total of 204 participants in 66 individual or group discussions across various organizations. Tables A.1 through A.4 provide an overview of the organizations we spoke with for the study, including the total number of representatives from each organization.

Interviews and discussions were completed either in person or by telephone. A minimum of two RAND researchers participated in each interview, with one researcher taking the lead in asking questions and the other researcher taking notes. In some cases, the interviews were with a single individual, and in other cases, we used more of a group-discussion format with multiple individuals from an organization in attendance during the session. We used a semistructured interview protocol for each interview or group discussion, with each protocol tailored to the purposes of each organization or individual with whom we spoke (e.g., questions focused on training for organizations responsible for training). The general topics and questions included the following:

- Broader understanding of human domain
  - What does the concept of human domain on a broader scale mean?
  - Who currently is doing human-domain-type work around the Air Force and/or joint environment?
  - Who should be doing and training in human-domain activities, to what level, and why? [Special operators, conventional forces, specific career fields, officers, enlisted, etc.]
- Development of human-domain concept
  - What was the process and reasoning behind the development of the human-domain concept?
  - Why do you think the process slowed?
  - Human domain versus human aspects of military operations (HAMO): Do you feel one term is more appropriate?
    - From your organization's perspective, is HAMO useful? Is it useful enough?
- Realms of human domain
  - If developed, what types of activities should policy or doctrine on human domain cover? [e.g., SC, operations, interoperability, SOF, cyber]
  - Why?
  - How does human domain enhance these activities?
- Human domain in your organization
  - What does the concept of human domain in your organization mean?
  - How do you use human-domain elements?
  - Where does human domain come into play in the planning and operations cycle for your organization? [e.g., planning, use of intel, tactical skills, etc.]
  - What are some of the major challenges you face using human domain in operations?
  - What doctrine, policy, or guidance is there that informs the use (or not) of human domain in your organization? [Get copies or citations if possible.]
  - What activities would a more uniform doctrine or policy on human domain help you with?
  - If your organization involves specialists in human-domain-type activities, how well are they integrated with conventional units, and why or why not?
- Training and integration of human domain
  - Does your organization conduct human-domain-type training?
    - For whom?
    - Describe it? [Length, topics covered.]
    - Is training progressive on a specific plan [so a Level 1, Level 2, that build on each other]?
    - What are the models you use for providing human-domain training?
    - How do you assess people's retention of the training objectives?
    - How do you assess the effectiveness of such training?

- What are some of the major challenges your organization faces in providing this kind of training?
- What more would you like to see in training?
  - Does your organization participate in training hosted by other organizations? How is human domain integrated into institutional and training events that your organization participates in [e.g., exercises, wargames]?

Tables A.1 through A.4 provide an overview of the organizations we spoke with for the study, including the total number of representatives from each organization.

Table A.1. U.S. Air Force Participants (Operations)

Organization	Number of Participants
Air Force Special Operations Command (AFSOC)	
Battlefield Airmen	8
Combat Aviation Advisors	10
A2 (Intel)	6
USAF Special Operations School	5
U.S. Air Force Headquarters (Air Staff)	
Operations, Plans, and Requirements (AF/A3)	5
Air Force Warfighting Integration Center (AFWIC)	1
Strategic Plans and Requirements (AF/A5S)	3
Intelligence, Surveillance, and Reconnaissance (AF/A2)	8
Security Cooperation (SC)	
Office of SC Iraq	1
818 Mobility Support and Advisory Squadron (MSAS)	5
Mobility Training Squadron	1
Secretary of the Air Force for International Affairs (SAF/IA)	8
United States Air Forces in Europe (USAFE)	3
United States Air Forces in Europe (USAFE)	
Contingency Branch	1
Medical Branch	2
USAFE Band	3
Air National Guard Component	1
USAFE Information Operations	1
Intelligence	
National Air and Space Intelligence Center (NASIC)	4
Air Mobility Command Intelligence Directorate	1
Cyber	
688th Cyberspace Wing	1
67th Cyberspace Wing	2

NOTE: We were not able to speak with representatives from Space Command.

Table A.2. U.S. Air Force Participants (Training and Education)

Organization	Number of Participants
U.S. Air Force Air Education and Training Command (AETC)	
AETC Headquarters	2
Special Missions Division (HQ AETC/A3Q)	5
The Professional Arms Center of Excellence (PACE)	3
Basic Military Training (BMT)	3
Air University	
Headquarters	2
LeMay Center for Doctrine Development and Education	2
International Officer School at Air University	1
International Officer Prep Program	1
Air War College	4
Inter-European Air Forces Academy (IEAFA)	8
Air Force Culture and Language Center (AFCLC)	3
Air Force Research Laboratory (AFRL)	2

Table A.3. Other U.S. Military Participants

Organization	Number of Participants
National Defense University	2
Office of the Secretary of Defense	1
Joint U.S. Military	
Special Operations Command	8
Strategic Plans and Policy (J5)	1
Joint Information Operations Warfare Center (JIOWC)	4
Army	
Special Operations Command (USASOC)	30
John F. Kennedy Special Warfare Center and School (SWCS)	4
Marine Corps Center for Advanced Operational Culture Learning	2

Table A.4. International Participants

International Military Partner	Number of Participants
United Kingdom	
Defence Cultural Specialist Unit (DCSU)	8
77th Brigade	10
Defence Geographic Center	8
Germany	
Bundeswehr Leadership Development and Civic Education Center	5
German Officer Candidacy School	6

Appendix B. Definition and Characteristics of a Warfighting Domain

The Joint Force currently recognizes five operational domains of warfare, which are also known as warfighting domains. Four of these domains—land, air, sea (also known as maritime), and space—encompass physical areas; and the fifth domain, cyberspace, includes global informational technology infrastructures and data (JP 3-0, 2017; JP 5-0, 2017). These domains have developed and received recognition over time, beginning with land and sea, then air, space, and—most recently—cyberspace (Allen and Gilbert, 2009). In this appendix, we review definitions of warfighting domains and key characteristics to assess the strengths and limitations of recognizing a sixth warfighting domain, namely, a human domain.

Definition of a Warfighting Domain

Different researchers and theorists have provided broad definitions or descriptions of what constitutes a warfighting domain. However, these are not widely agreed on and have not been commonly accepted within military doctrine. A small set of these domain descriptions include, for example:

- "The sphere[s] of interest and influence in which activities, functions, and operations are undertaken to accomplish missions and exercise control over an opponent in order to achieve desired effects" (Allen and Gilbert, 2009)
- "Mediums (or portions thereof) of strategic significance requiring the development of specific assets to explore, exploit, and control them. They are essentially social constructs" (Dupuy, 2013)
- "'[Territories] over which rule or control is exercised.' These operational environments are warfighting domains which represent physical expressions where military operations are conducted; where Joint Force Commanders contest for enemy dominance" (Kelly, 2008).

Generally, descriptions of warfighting domains appear to emphasize unique spheres of interest and influence within each domain. In addition, descriptions also highlight the possibility for allies and adversaries to operate within these domain spaces. In other words, they propose that domains encompass spaces in which battles for control may occur. Although these were initially conceptualized as easily identifiable physical spaces (e.g., land, sea, air, space), establishment of the cyberspace domain broadened considerations regarding what might constitute a domain (e.g., Chilton, 2009).

Characteristics of a Warfighting Domain

Notably, joint military doctrine defines characteristics of each of the five contemporary warfighting domains (e.g., Joint Staff Joint Force Development [J7], 2016). However, just as there is no single definition or description of a warfighting domain, there is no agreed-on delineation of the characteristics of warfighting domains, more broadly (Cornelius, 2015). This lack of clearly identified and commonly accepted characteristics of warfighting domains appears to contribute to debates regarding the recognition of new domains. For example, many questioned whether cyberspace should be recognized as a warfighting domain, due to differing theories and judgments on domain characteristics (Libicki, 2012; McGuffin and Mitchell, 2014; Songip et al., 2013). Table B.1 lists several characteristics that a number of observers have used when referencing warfighting domains and details how these apply to traditional domains as well as a human domain. We describe each of them in more depth in the sections to follow.

Capabilities

One element some observers use to differentiate warfighting domains encompasses the presence of domain-specific capabilities. These capabilities can include the existence of equipment central to that specific domain and practitioners that have received training on how to operate within the domain (Chilton, 2009; Denning, 2015; USSOCOM, 2015). For example, aircraft are a central component to the air domain, and pilots are required to operate these aircraft. Similarly, although it does not have an easily identifiable physical space, computers and internet access are central to the cyberspace domain, and cyberspace operators are required to ensure effective functioning within the cyber domain (Allen and Gilbert, 2009). The human domain might place less emphasis on physical spaces or equipment, instead focusing on the skills necessary to maneuver across the human terrain and interact with others, which might require individuals with extensive training in the behavioral and social sciences (Gregg, 2016).

However, one could argue that many military capabilities are fungible across domains, or at least provide direct support to multiple domains. For example, an F-15E Strike Eagle can fire an antisatellite weapon into space, shoot down an adversary fighter in the air, fire an antiship missile at a ship at sea, bomb a tank in a conventional war on land, be used to help train allied air forces, or bomb an insurgent on land. Many observers contend that of all so-called capabilities, human-focused capabilities are the most fungible.

Resources

Related to capabilities, resources must exist to maintain and improve capabilities within a domain (Brandes, 2013). Resources influence capabilities and may be considered a component of capabilities. In other words, the tools and training resources that form the capabilities must be well managed and continuously updated (Chilton, 2009). Therefore, the existence of aircraft and trained pilots might form the basis of air domain capabilities. However, resources must be

Table B.1. Commonly Cited Considerations for Warfighting Domain Description and Differentiation

Characteristic	Example Application to Traditional Domains	Example Application to a Human Domain
Capabilities: There are domain-specific capabilities, including skilled practitioners trained on how to operate in the domain	• Land: land systems; soldiers • Sea: ships; sailors • Air: aircraft; pilots • Space: satellites; space operators • Cyberspace: computers; internet; cyber operators	Language, cultural, and communication skills; behavioral and social scientists (including psychologists, anthropologists, sociologists)
Resources: Sufficient tools and resources are available to operate in the domain	• Continuously updated and maintained operating systems and improved training for domain operators to permit effective functioning within domain	Continuously updated information regarding how individuals and groups think and act, both generally and in different geographic locations, which would need to be communicated in training
Actors: Opposing forces must be possible in the domain. It is an area in which not only nonhostile civilians operate	• Combatants exist within each domain, and weaponization of devices within each domain has occurred or is possible	Combatants can influence and persuade people and groups to act as adversaries
Strategy: Military strategies and rules of engagement for how to operate exist	• Strategies for operating offensively and defensively in each domain; rules and/or guidance regarding targets and appropriate military actions within the domain	Strategies may include techniques for conducting human-domain analyses and creating and countering influence campaigns
Control and Influence: One side must be able to dominate an opposing force within the domain	• In each domain, it is possible for one force to hold dominance or majority control of a space or capability	Ability to influence specified individuals and groups with more efficacy than an enemy/adversary
Centralized Command: There is a centralized command that focuses on actions taken within that domain	• Land: Army • Sea: Navy • Air: Air Force • Space: Air Force Space Command • Cyberspace: Cyber Command	Centralized command does not currently exist
Structure: A domain is not fully encompassed in one other domain	• Capabilities, mission, and influence techniques are unique within environment	Discussion ongoing regarding structure
Permanence: The domain has relative permanence	• Rapid malleability of total domain is not possible	Specific behaviors and social contexts can change rapidly. Basic human psychological and social processes do not change rapidly
Synergy and Assistance: Domain provides opportunities for synergies with other domains	• Capabilities work in synergy with other domains, and capabilities in a domain can be used to help those in another domain fight an opposing force	Information collection/sharing and influence operations can support other domains

invested to continuously update aircraft and advance pilot training. In a human domain, information regarding the psychological and social (including cultural) processes of individuals and groups would need to be continuously updated, and operators would need to receive regularly updated training on these processes.

Actors

The existence of, or potential for the existence of, opposing forces operating within the domain is another characteristic of warfighting domains (Allen and Gilbert, 2009; Denning, 2015; Hollon, 2012). In a human domain, this might involve combatants informing and influencing individuals and groups to operate as adversaries against the United States and its allies, with the United States operating its own influence campaigns (Gregg, 2016; Schnell, 2014).

Strategy

If adversaries are a necessary component to a warfighting domain, then strategies for addressing those adversaries are also needed (Brandes, 2013; Dermer, 2013). Another characteristic of a warfighting domain, therefore, is the existence of coordinated military strategies and rules of engagement that address operations within the specified domain (Brandes, 2013). Strategies include, for example, identification of valid and lawful military targets, addressing what constitutes an act of war, and gathering information regarding offensive and defensive military actions. In the human domain, strategies might include techniques for conducting human-domain analyses and creating and countering influence campaigns (Sands, 2013).

Control and Influence

Part of military strategy is establishing or understanding how one might achieve control and influence within the domain, so attaining control and exerting influence might be considered parts of a military strategy. Building from this, an additional characteristic of warfighting domains, which might be considered an element of strategy, appears to be the ability for one force, or side, to dominate and hold control over another force within each domain (Allen and Gilbert, 2009). For example, in the air domain, this encompasses the ability for one actor or group of actors to hold air superiority. In the human domain, control and influence has been conceptualized as the ability for an entity to more effectively influence certain individuals and groups than another entity (Gregg, 2016).

Centralized Command

To coordinate domain capabilities, identify and address actors within the domain, and develop and disseminate strategy, command is needed. As such, an additional characteristic noted when addressing warfighting domains is a centralized command for each domain (Allen and Gilbert, 2009; Lynn, 2010). Although other organizations may operate within and assist with actions taken in a domain, one command holds primary responsibility for oversight and coordination of that domain. For domains recognized by the U.S. military, the U.S. Army, Navy, and Air Force hold primary responsibility for the land, sea, and air domains, respectively. Air Force Space Command holds primary responsibility for the space domain, and Cyber Command addresses the cyberspace domain. One organization or command does not currently exist for the human domain. If one were to be established, consideration would need to be given to coordination across the services (Samaan, 2010).

Structure

Another relatively abstract characteristic discussed in the context of warfighting domains involves structure relative to other domains. For example, to be considered a warfighting domain, one proposition is that a domain should not be fully encompassed within another domain, so it should have capabilities and functions specific to an environment (Allen and Gilbert, 2009). However, it may operate in conjunction with—supportive of and supported by actions in—other domains. Applying this concept to the most recently established domain, the cyberspace domain gives and receives information and capabilities to the other domains. However, it is not fully encompassed within, for example, only the land domain.

The extent to which the human domain is unique from the current warfighting domains remains the topic of ongoing discussion. The human domain has been described as a unique domain, a component of the land domain, and a function across several domains (Cornelius, 2015). If conceptualized as a component of another domain or simply as a function across domains, then the human domain might not be considered a different warfighting domain. By contrast, if it is thought of as encompassing distinctive capabilities that can be applied to population-centric battles, then the human domain might more closely align with the essence of a separate warfighting domain, and as such, it might be worthy of separate inclusion in the structure of warfighting domains. However, moving beyond whether a human domain possesses the structural essence of a general warfighting domain, strategists and operators must also consider whether a separate human domain would help, hinder, or have no effect on comprehension, engagement, and effect (Cornelius, 2015; Libicki, 2012).

Permanence

Relative permanence is an additional characteristic discussed in the context of warfighting domains (Denning, 2015; McGuffin and Mitchell, 2014). Although humans can change characteristics of traditional domains, such as geography, it is difficult, costly, and time-consuming to do so (Denning, 2015). Similarly, elements of the cyberspace domain are not permanent, but operation requirements, software, regulations, and so forth do not completely change within an extremely limited time frame. For the human domain, certain behaviors and social contexts may change rapidly (Gergen, 1973). However, many psychological, social, and behavioral aspects remain consistent over time (Schlenker, 1974).

Synergy and Asymmetric Assistance Across Domains

The ability for a domain to operate in synergy with other warfighting domains and to provide asymmetric aid to operations occurring in other domains are also considered key characteristics of a warfighting domain (Allen and Gilbert, 2009). For example, the capabilities of the air domain can provide support to and work in synergy with operations in the land domain. Applying these concepts to a human domain, the abilities to collect information from targeted individuals and groups and to influence actions taken in support of allies and against enemies can operate in synergy with and support the operations of other domains (Celeski, 2014).

Summary

Although doctrinal definitions of separate warfighting domains exist, a well-known, agreed-on definition of what constitutes a warfighting domain, more broadly, does not exist. In theory, several of the characteristics described above would support the idea of a human domain, but others—including centralized command, structure, and permanence—are less clear in their applicability to the establishment of a human domain. This lack of clarity regarding a definition and key characteristics makes establishing a new joint warfighting domain around human aspects of military operations challenging.

Bibliography

363rd Intelligence Surveillance Reconnaissance Group Operating Instruction, Volume 1, Unit Intelligence Training, January 6, 2016.

AFCLC—*See* Air Force Culture and Language Center.

AFDD—*See* Air Force Doctrine Documents (various).

AFECD—*See* Air Force Personnel Center, *Air Force Enlisted Classification Directory*.

AFMC—*See* Air Force Materiel Command.

AFPD—*See* Air Force Policy Directives (various).

AFRL—*See* Air Force Research Lab.

Air Force, *Basic Doctrine*, Volume I, February 27, 2015. As of February 8, 2018: http://www.doctrine.af.mil/Core-Doctrine/Vol-1-Basic-Doctrine/

Air Force Annex 3-0, *Operations and Planning*, November 4, 2016. As of February 18, 2018: http://www.doctrine.af.mil/Portals/61/documents/Annex_3-0/3-0-Annex-OPERATIONS -PLANNING.pdf

Air Force Culture and Language Center, "Cross-Cultural Competence Fact Sheet," Maxwell AFB, Ala.: Air Force Culture and Language Center, 2017. As of July 25, 2018: https://www.airuniversity.af.edu/Portals/10/AFCLC/documents/library/3C%20Fact %20Sheet.pdf?ver=2018-11-01-151005-553

Air Force Culture and Language Center, "Our Story," webpage, May 1, 2018. As of February 12, 2018: http://culture.af.mil/our-story.html

Air Force Doctrine Document 1-1, *Leadership and Force Development*, Washington, D.C.: Headquarters, U.S. Air Force, 2011.

Air Force Doctrine Document 2-0, *Global Integrated Intelligence, Surveillance, and Reconnaissance Operations*, January 6, 2012. As of April 16, 2018: https://fas.org/irp/doddir/usaf/afdd2-0.pdf

Air Force Instruction 36-4001, *Air Force Language, Regional Expertise and Culture Program*, September 2, 2014. As of February 10, 2018: http://static.e-publishing.af.mil/production/1/af_a1/publication/afi36-4001/afi36-4001.pdf

Air Force Materiel Command, "AFMC History," webpage, April 26, 2017. As of February 10, 2018:
http://www.afmc.af.mil/Home/Welcome/

Air Force Materiel Command, "AFMC Mission," webpage, April 26, 2017. As of February 10, 2018:
http://www.afmc.af.mil/Home/Welcome/

Air Force Personnel Center, *Air Force Enlisted Classification Directory*, United States Air Force, October 31, 2017.

Air Force Policy Directive 36-26, *Total Force Development and Management*, Washington, D.C.: Headquarters, U.S. Air Force, 2015.

Air Force Policy Directive 36-40, *Air Force Language, Regional Expertise, and Culture Program*, August 7, 2018. As of February 25, 2020:
https://static.e-publishing.af.mil/production/1/af_a1/publication/afpd36-40/afpd36-40.pdf

Air Force Public Affairs, "Air Force Opens Space Training to Allies, Accelerates Space Acquisition," Colorado Springs, Colo., April 18, 2018. As of June 21, 2018:
http://www.af.mil/News/Article-Display/Article/1496222/air-force-opens-space-training-to-allies-accelerates-space-acquisition/

Air Force Research Lab Information Directorate, website, January 23, 2018. As of February 12, 2018:
http://www.wpafb.af.mil/Portals/60/documents/afrl/ri/afrl-ri-facilities-180123.pdf?ver=2018-01-23-100818-810

Air Force Space Command, *High Frontier*, special issue: *International Space*, Vol. 6 No. 2, February 2010. As of June 21, 2018:
http://www.afspc.af.mil/Portals/3/documents/HF/AFD-100226-085.pdf

Air National Guard, "Cryptologic Language Analyst," webpage, 2018. As of May 21, 2018:
https://www.goang.com/careers/cryptologic-language-analyst/1n3x1

Air University, *Air Force Culture and Language Center*, undated. As of February 27, 2020:
https://www.airuniversity.af.edu/AFCLC/About/

Air University, "Air University Curtis E. LeMay Center for Doctrine Development and Education," webpage, April 27, 2017. As of February 10, 2018:
http://www.au.af.mil/au/lemay/main.htm

Air University, "U.S. Air Force Wargaming Gateway," webpage, June 11, 2017b. As of February 10, 2018:
http://www.airuniversity.af.mil/lemay/display/article/1099721/us-air-force-wargaming-gateway-mil-only/

Aleva, D., J. Ianni, and V. Schmidt, *Space Situation Awareness: Human Research Trends,* Wright-Patterson Air Force Base, Ohio: Air Force Research Laboratory, 2010.

Alford, Lewis E., and Brian A. Dudas, *Developing a Validation Methodology for TacAir Soar Agents in EAAGLES,* graduate research project, Wright-Patterson Air Force Base, Ohio: Air Force Institute of Technology, May 2005.

Allen, Dr. Patrick D., and Dennis P. Gilbert, Jr., "The Information Sphere Domain Increasing Understanding and Cooperation,*"* In C. Czosseck and K. Geers (Eds.) *The Virtual Battlefield: Perspectives on Cyber Warfare,* IOS Press, pp: 132–142, 2009. Accessed at: https://books.google.com/books?hl=en&lr=&id=BKDbN5eUhV0C&oi=fnd&pg=PA132 &dq=The+Information+Sphere+Domain:+Increasing+Understanding+and+Cooperation &ots=v3K-vnXscN&sig=8HoDqfoZ4ZDDLilXk8wHhc2F5Xw#v=onepage&q=The%20 Information%20Sphere%20Domain%3A%20Increasing%20Understanding%20and%20 Cooperation&f=false

Allied Joint Doctrine for Operational-Level Planning (AJP-5), NATO, 2013. As of June 13, 2018:
https://assets.publishing.service.gov.uk/government/uploads/system/uploads/attachment _data/file/787263/archive_doctrine_nato_op_planning_ajp_5_with_UK_elements.pdf

Annex 2-0, *Global Integrated ISR Operations,* January 29, 2015. As of April 20, 2018:
http://www.doctrine.af.mil/Portals/61/documents/Annex_2-0/2-0-Annex-GLOBAL -INTEGRATED-ISR.pdf?ver=2017-09-18-174804-620

Annex 3-2 Irregular Warfare, *Air Force Capabilities and IW Execution,* July 12, 2016. As of April 23, 2018:
http://www.doctrine.af.mil/Portals/61/documents/Annex_3-2/3-2-D07-IW-AF-IW-Capability .pdf?ver=2017-09-19-153859-050

Army Modeling and Simulation Office, "Organization Wire Diagram," webpage, undated. As of June 20, 2018:
http://www.ms.army.mil/org-wire-diagram.html

Army War College, "Strategic Wargaming Series," wargaming brochure, March 2015. As of June 19, 2018:
http://www.csl.army.mil/LCDW/StrategicWargamingDivision/publications/USAWC %20Wargaming%20Brochure%20March%202015.pdf

Arwood, Sam, *Cyberspace as a Theater of Conflict: Federal Law, National Strategy and the Departments of Defense and Homeland Security,* thesis, Wright-Patterson Air Force Base, Ohio: AFIT, 2007.

Astorino-Courtois, Allison, ed., *A Cognitive Capabilities Agenda: A Multi-Step Approach for Closing DoD's Cognitive Capability Gap*, Strategic Multilayer Assessment White Paper, 2017.

Babcock, Chris, "Preparing for the Cyber Battleground of the Future," *Air and Space Power Journal*, November–December 2015, pp. 61–73.

Bada, Maria, Angela M. Sasse, and Jason R. C. Nurse, *Cyber Security Awareness Campaigns: Why do they fail to change behavior?*, January 2015. Accessed on February 27, 2020: https://arxiv.org/ftp/arxiv/papers/1901/1901.02672.pdf

Barford, P., M. Dacier, T. G. Dietterich, M. Fredrikson, J. Giffin, S. Jajodia, S. Jha, J. Li, P. Liu, P. Ning, X. Ou, D. Song, L. Strater, V. Swarup, G. Tadda, C. Wang, and J. Yen, "Cyber SA: Situational Awareness for Cyber Defense," in Sushil Jajodia, Peng Liu, Vipin Swarup, Cliff Wang, eds., *Cyber Situation Awareness*, New York: Springer, 2010.

Bestard, Jaime J., "Air Force Research Laboratory Innovation: Pushing the Envelope in Analytical Wargaming," *Journal of Cyber Security and Information Systems*, Vol. 4, No. 3., November 2016, pp. 12–13. As of June 19, 2018: https://www.csiac.org/journal-article/air- force-research-laboratory-innovation-pushing-the -envelope-in-analytical-wargaming/

Brandes, Sean, "The Newest Warfighting Domain: Cyberspace," *SYNESIS: A Journal of Science, Technology, Ethics, and Policy*, 2013, pp. 90–95.

Campaign Execution, Joint Doctrine Publication 3-00, 3rd ed., Swindon, UK: Development, Concepts and Doctrine Centre, 2012. As of June 13, 2018: https://assets.publishing.service.gov.uk/government/uploads/system/uploads/attachment _data/file/43329/20120829jdp300_ed3_ch1.pdf

Celeski, Joseph D., "SOF, the Human Domain and the Conduct of Campaigns," *Special Warfare*, Vol. 27, No. 3, 2014, pp. 5–9.

Chairman of the Joint Chiefs of Staff, *Joint and National Intelligence Support to Military Operations,* Joint Publication 2-01. As of August 7, 2020: https://www.jcs.mil/Portals/36/Documents/Doctrine/pubs/jp2_01_20170705v2.pdf

Chairman of the Joint Chiefs of Staff Instruction, *Language, Regional Expertise, and Culture (LREC) Capability Identification, Planning, and Sourcing*, 3126.01A, January 31, 2013.

Cheng, Dean, "China's Military Role in Space," *Strategic Studies Quarterly*, Spring 2012, pp. 55–77.

Chilton, Kevin P., "Cyberspace Leadership: Towards New Culture, Conduct, and Capabilities," *Air and Space Journal*, 2009, pp. 5–10.

CJSCI—*See* Chairman of the Joint Chiefs of Staff Instruction.

Cleaver, Hannah, "German Soldiers Desecrate Afghan Skull," *The Telegraph*, October 26, 2006. As of June 2, 2020:
https://www.telegraph.co.uk/news/worldnews/1532448/German-soldiers-desecrate-Afghan -skull.html

Cleveland, Charles, Benjamin Jensen, Susan Bryant, and Arnel David, *Military Strategy in the 21st Century: People, Connectivity, and Competition*, Amherst, N.Y.: Cambria Press, 2018.

Connable, Ben, "Human Terrain System Is Dead, Long Live . . . What? Building and Sustaining Military Cultural Competence in the Aftermath of the Human Terrain System," *Military Review*, January–February 2018. As of June 14, 2018:
https://www.armyupress.army.mil/Journals/Military-Review/English-Edition-Archives/ January-February-2018/Human-Terrain-System-is-Dead-Long-Live-What/

Connable, Ben, Jason H. Campbell, and Dan Madden, *Stretching and Exploiting Thresholds for High-Order War: How Russia, China, and Iran Are Eroding American Influence Using Time-Tested Measures Short of War*, Santa Monica, Calif.: RAND Corporation, RR-1003-A, 2016. As of November 3, 2019:
https://www.rand.org/pubs/research_reports/RR1003.html

Connable, Ben, Michael J. McNerney, William Marcellino, Aaron Frank, Henry Hargrove, Marek N. Posard, S. Rebecca Zimmerman, Natasha Lander, Jasen J. Castillo, and James Sladden, *Will to Fight: Analyzing, Modeling, and Simulating the Will to Fight of Military Units*, Santa Monica, Calif.: RAND Corporation, RR-2341-A, 2018. As of October 23, 2019:
https://www.rand.org/pubs/research_reports/RR2341.html

Cornelius, Robert L., *An Evaluation of the Human Domain Concept: Organizing the Knowledge, Influence, and Activity in Population-Centric Warfare*, Fort Leavenworth, Kan.: Army Command and General Staff College, 2015. As of December 12, 2017:
http://www.dtic.mil/dtic/tr/fulltext/u2/1007869.pdf

Coyer, Paul, "Chinese Information Warfare: Leveraging the Power of Perception," *Forbes*, October 13, 2015. As of July 2, 2018:
https://www.forbes.com/sites/paulcoyer/2015/10/13/chinese-information-warfare-and-sino -american-rivalry/#59fac103703b

Cragin, Kim, Kathleen Reedy, Beth Grill, Matthew Carroll, Phillip Padilla, William Marcellino, Joshua Mendelsohn, Andrew Cady, Madeline Magnuson, and Zachary Haldeman, *Hide and Seek: Interpreting Human Behavior from an ISR Environment*, Santa Monica, Calif.: RAND Corporation, 2017, Not available to the general public.

Cuevas, Haydee M, "Mitigating the Negative Effects of Stress in Space Flight: A Transactional Approach," *Journal of Human Performance in Extreme Environments*, Vol. 7, No. 2, 2003, pp. 69–77.

Culture and Human Terrain, Joint Doctrine Note 4/13, Swindon, UK: Development, Concepts and Doctrine Centre, 2013. As of June 13, 2018:
https://assets.publishing.service.gov.uk/government/uploads/system/uploads/attachment _data/file/256043/20131008-_JDN_4_13_Culture-U.pdf

Davis, Rochelle, "Culture as a Weapon System," *Middle East Report*, Summer 2010.

Day of Geography, "A Day in the Life of the UK Defence Geographic Centre," webpage, November 17, 2014. As of June 13, 2018:
http://www.dayofgeography.com/?p=756

Defense Science Board Task Force, "Understanding Human Dynamics," March 2011. As of February 10, 2018:
https://www.hsdl.org/?view&did=38172

Denning, Dorothy E., "Rethinking the Cyber Domain and Deterrence," *Joint Forces Quarterly*, 2015, pp. 8–15.

Department of the Army, Field Manual 3-24/Marine Corps Warfighting Publication 3-33.5, *Insurgencies and Countering Insurgencies*, May 13, 2014.

Department of Defense, *The Department of Defense Cyber Strategy*, April 17, 2015. As of June 18, 2018:
https://www.defense.gov/Portals/1/features/2015/0415_cyber-strategy/Final_2015_DoD _CYBER_STRATEGY_for_web.pdf

Department of Defense, *Defense Modeling and Simulation Coordination Center*. As of February 27, 2020:
https://www.msco.mil/

Department of Defense, *Strategy for Operations in the Information Environment*, June 2016. As of May 24, 2018:
https://www.defense.gov/Portals/1/Documents/pubs/DoD-Strategy-for- Operations-in-the-IE -Signed-20160613.pdf

Department of Defense, *Summary of the 2018 National Defense Strategy of the United States of America: Sharpening the American Military's Competitive Edge*, Washington, D.C., 2018.

Department of Defense Directive 5000.59, *DoD Modeling and Simulation (M&S) Management*, August 8, 2007. As of June 18, 2018:
http://www.esd.whs.mil/Portals/54/Documents/DD/issuances/dodd/500059p.pdf

Department of Defense Instruction 5000.70, *Management of DoD Modeling and Simulation (M&S) Activities*, May 10, 2012 (incorporating "Change 3," October 15, 2018). As of June 17, 2018:
https://www.esd.whs.mil/Portals/54/Documents/DD/issuances/dodi/500070p.pdf?ver=2018 -11-07-101418-490

85

Dermer, James B., Cyber *Warfare: New Character with Strategic Results*, thesis, Carlisle, Pa.: United States Army War College, 2013.

Doctrine for the Armed Forces of the United States, *Joint Publication 1*, Incorporating Change 1 July 12, 2017. As of March 25, 2013:
https://www.jcs.mil/Portals/36/Documents/Doctrine/pubs/jp1_ch1.pdf

DoD—*See* Department of Defense.

DoDD—*See* Department of Defense Directive.

DoDI—*See* Department of Defense Instruction.

Dstl, webpage of the Defence Science and Technology Laboratory, Gov.UK, 2018. As of June 13, 2018:
https://www.gov.uk/government/organisations/defence-science-and-technology-laboratory

Dupuy, William, *On Glitchkriege: Strategy in the Cyber-Age*, Maxwell Air Force Base, Ala.: Air University, 2013.

Finney, Nathan, *Human Terrain Team Handbook*, United States Army, September 2008. As of February 12, 2018:
https://info.publicintelligence.net/humanterrainhandbook.pdf

FM 3-24—*See* Department of the Army, Field Manual 3-24.

Footsoldier, David Hume, "Introducing 77 Brigade and a New Way of Business," *ThinkDefence*, blog, February 19, 2015. As of June 13, 2018:
https://www.thinkdefence.co.uk/2015/02/introducing-77-brigade-new-way-business/

"Gendarmerie of the Air," National Gendarmerie, Ministry of the Interior. As of June 12, 2018:
https://www.gendarmerie.interieur.gouv.fr/Notre-institution/Nos- composantes/Gendarmeries -specialisees/Gendarmerie-de-l-air

Gergen, Kenneth J., "Social Psychology as History," *Journal of Personality and Social Psychology*, Vol. 26, No. 2, 1973, pp. 309–320.

Grady, John, "Panel: Russia and China Practicing More Hybrid, Information Warfare," *USNI News*, March 22, 2017. As of July 2, 2018:
https://news.usni.org/2017/03/22/panel-russia- china-practicing-hybrid-information-warfare

Green Sands, Robert R., "Thinking Differently: Unlocking the Human Domain in Support of the 21st Century Intelligence Mission, *Small Wars Journal,* pp. 1–43, August 2013.

Gregg, Heather, "The Human Domain and Influence Operations in the 21st Century," *Special Operations Journal*, Vol. 2, No. 2, 2016, pp. 92–105.

Grier, Rebecca A., Bruce Skarin, Alexander Lubyansky, and Lawrence Wolpert, "SCIPR: A Computational Model to Simulate Cultural Identities for Predicting Reactions to Events." Presented at the Second International Conference on Computational Cultural Dynamics, University of Maryland, College Park, Md., September 2008.

Gustafson, Kathryn, *Culture, Language Center Staff Launches Culture-General Training*, Air Force Culture, Region and Language Program Office, February 26, 2010. As of February 11, 2018:
http://www.afpc.af.mil/News/Article-Display/Article/422972/culture-language-center-staff -launches-culture-general-training/

Hagel, Chuck, U.S. Secretary of Defense, Department of Defense, "The Defense Innovation Initiative," memorandum for Department of Defense leadership, Washington, D.C., November 15, 2014.

Harrison, Albert A., "Humanizing Outer Space: Architecture, Habitability, and Behavioral Health," *Acta Astronautica*, Vol. 66, 2010, pp. 890–896.

Headquarters Department of the Army, *Army Special Operations Forces*, FM 3-05 (FM 100-25), September 2006.

Headquarters Department of the Army, *Department of the Army ADRP 3-0 Operations*, October 2017.

Headquarters, Department of the Army Headquarters, United States Marine Corps, *Intelligence Preparation of the Battlefield/Battlespace*, MCRP 2-10B.1, November 2014.

Headquarters United States Marine Corps, *Small Wars Manual*, Washington, D.C., [1940] 1990.

Herbert, Mark, "The Human Domain: The Army's Necessary Squishiness," *Military Review*, 2014, pp. 81–87.

Hillson, R., "The DIME/PMESII Model Suite Requirements Project," *NRL Review*, 2009.

Hockey, G. R. J., *Human Performance in Extended Space Operations*, Report of ESA Topical Team in Psychology, November 2011.

Hollon, Cory S., *New Domain, New Direction*, thesis, Maxwell Air Force Base, Ala.: Air Command and Staff College, April 2012.

Hosmer, Stephen T., *Psychological Effects of U.S. Air Operations in Four Wars*, Santa Monica, Calif.: RAND Corporation, MR-576-AF, 1996. As of October 23, 2019:
https://www.rand.org/pubs/monograph_reports/MR576.html

Hurley, W. J., C. R. Bucher, S. K. Numrich, S. M. Ouellette, J. B. Resnick, *Non-Kinetic Capabilities for Irregular Warfare: Four Case Studies*, Institute for Defense Analyses, March 2009. As of June 8, 2018:
www.dtic.mil/get-tr-doc/pdf?AD=ADA501354

Insinna, Valeria, "Air Force Looks to Ramp Up Space Training, Info Sharing with Allies," *DefenseNews*, April 18, 2018. As of June 21, 2018:
https://www.defensenews.com/digital-show-dailies/space-symposium/2018/04/18/air-force
-looks-to-ramp-up-space-training-info-sharing-with-international-partners/

Iwig, Chelsea, Carolyn Newton, Eric Watkins, Gisela Munoz, Noah Feaster, Amy Seo, Carlos Giraldo, Jason Kring, "Human Factors and Behavioral Research at a Mars Analog Habitat," *Proceedings of the Human Factors and Ergonomic Society 57th Annual Meeting*, 2013.

JC-HAMO—*See* Joint Chiefs of Staff, *Joint Concept for Human Aspects of Military Operations*.

JIOWC—*See* Joint Information Operations Warfare Center.

Joint Chiefs of Staff, *Joint Concept for Human Aspects of Military Operations (JC-HAMO)*, October 19, 2016.

Joint Chiefs of Staff, *Joint Concept for Integrated Campaigning*, March 16, 2018a. As of May 24, 2018:
http://www.jcs.mil/Portals/36/Documents/Doctrine/concepts/joint_concept_integrated
_campaign.pdf?ver=2018-03-28-102833-257

Joint Chiefs of Staff, *Joint Concept for Operating in the Information Environment (JCOIE)*, July 28, 2018b. As of June 3, 2020:
https://www.jcs.mil/Portals/36/Documents/Doctrine/concepts/joint_concepts_jcoie.pdf
?ver=2018-08-01-142119-830

Joint Chiefs of Staff, Joint Publication 1, *Doctrine for the Armed Forces of the United States, Incorporating Change 1*, July 12, 2017. As of July 2, 2018:
https://www.jcs.mil/Portals/36/Documents/Doctrine/pubs/jp1_ch1.pdf

Joint Chiefs of Staff, Joint Publication 2-0, *Joint Intelligence*, October 22, 2013. As of April 16, 2018:
http://www.jcs.mil/Portals/36/Documents/Doctrine/pubs/jp2_0.pdf

Joint Chiefs of Staff, Joint Publication 2-01.3, *Joint Intelligence Preparation of the Operational Environment*, May 21, 2014. As of June 14, 2018:
https://fas.org/irp/doddir/dod/jp2-01- 3.pdf

Joint Chiefs of Staff, Joint Publication 3-0, *Joint Operations*, January 17, 2017. As of December 12, 2017:
http://www.dtic.mil/doctrine/new_pubs/jp3_0.pdf

Joint Chiefs of Staff, Joint Publication 3-06, *Joint Urban Operations*, November 20, 2013. As of June 14, 2018:
https://www.jcs.mil/Portals/36/Documents/Doctrine/pubs/jp3_06.pdf

Joint Chiefs of Staff, Joint Publication 3-07, *Stability*, August 3, 2016. As of June 14, 2018:
http://www.jcs.mil/Portals/36/Documents/Doctrine/pubs/jp3_07.pdf

Joint Chiefs of Staff, Joint Publication 3-13.2, *Military Information Support Operations*, December 20, 2011. As of April 22, 2020:
https://jfsc.ndu.edu/Portals/72/Documents/JC2IOS/Additional_Reading/1C1_JP_3-13-2.pdf

Joint Chiefs of Staff, Joint Publication 3-24, *Counterinsurgency*, April 25, 2018c. As of June 14, 2018:
http://www.jcs.mil/Portals/36/Documents/Doctrine/pubs/jp3_24.pdf

Joint Chiefs of Staff, Joint Publication 5-0, *Joint Operation Planning*, June 16, 2017. As of December 12, 2017:
http://www.dtic.mil/doctrine/new_pubs/jp5_0_20171606.pdf

Joint Information Operations Warfare Center, "The Athena Simulation: Modeling and Social Cultural Landscape," briefing, May 17, 2016.

Joint Special Operations University, "JSOU Courses," 2018. As of June 18, 2018:
https://www.socom.mil/JSOU/Pages/JSOUCourses.aspx

Joint Staff Joint Force Development (J7), *Cross-Domain Synergy in Joint Operations: Planner's Guide*, January 14, 2016. As of December 12, 2017:
https://www.jcs.mil/Portals/36/Documents/Doctrine/concepts/cross_domain_planning_guide .pdf?ver=2017-12-28-161956-230

Jones, Randolph M., John E. Laird, Paul E. Nielsen, Karen J. Coulter, Patrick Kenny, Frank V. Koss, "Automated Intelligent Pilots for Combat Flight Simulation," *AI Magazine*, March 1, 1999, pp. 27–41.

Jones, Seth, and Arturo Munoz, *Afghanistan's Local War: Building Local Defense Forces*, Santa Monica, Calif.: RAND Corporation, MG-1002-MCIA, 2010. As of October 23, 2019:
https://www.rand.org/pubs/monographs/MG1002.html

JP—*See* Joint Chiefs of Staff, Joint Publications (various).

JSOU—*See* Joint Special Operations University.

Kanas, Nick A., Vyacheslav P. Salnitskiy, Jennifer E. Boyd, Vadim I. Gushin, Daniel S. Weiss, Stephanie A. Saylor, Olga P. Kozerenko, and Charles R. Marmar, "Crewmember and Mission Control Personnel Interactions During International Space Station Missions," *Aviation, Space, and Environmental Medicine*, Vol. 78, No. 6, 2007, pp. 601–607.

Kanas, Nick, Vyacheslav Salnitskiy, Ellen M. Grund, Vadim Gushin, Daniel S. Weiss, Olga Kozerenko, Alexander Sled, and Charles R. Marmar, "Social and Cultural Issues During Shuttle/Mir Space Missions," *Acta Astronautica*, Vol. 47, 2000, pp. 647–655.

Karnow, Stanley, "Ho Chi Minh: He Married Nationalism to Communism and Perfected the Deadly Art of Guerrilla Warfare," *Time*, April 13, 1998. As of April 22, 2020:
http://content.time.com/time/magazine/article/0,9171,988162,00.html

Kauffman, Brent A., "The Human Elements of Military Operations," workshop, January 13–14, 2015, Center for Strategic Leadership, October 14, 2015. As of June 18, 2018: http://www.csl.army.mil/LCDW/StrategicWargamingDivision/publications/Human%20Elements%20Workshop%20Report.pdf

Kelly, Olen L., *Cyberspace Domain: A Warfighting Substantiated Operational Environment Imperative*, Carlisle, Pa.: U.S. Army War College, March 15, 2008.

Knott, Benjamin, *Cyber Trust and Influence.* Presented at Proceedings of the Human Factors and Ergonomics Society Annual Meeting, October 2014. As of April 12, 2018: https://journals.sagepub.com/doi/pdf/10.1177/1541931214581085

Land Operations, Army Doctrine Publication AC 71940, Bristol, UK: Ministry of Defence, 2017. As of June 13, 2018: https://assets.publishing.service.gov.uk/government/uploads/system/uploads/attachment_data/file/605298/Army_Field_Manual__AFM__A5_Master_ADP_Interactive_Gov_Web.pdf

Lee, Caitlin, Bart E. Bennett, Lisa M. Harrington, and Darrell D. Jones, *Rare Birds: Understanding and Addressing Air Force Underrepresentation in Senior Joint Positions in the Post–Goldwater Nichols Era*, Santa Monica, Calif.: RAND Corporation, RR-2089-AF, 2017. As of October 23, 2019: https://www.rand.org/pubs/research_reports/RR2089.html

Lee, Sangkuk, "China's 'Three Warfares': Origins, Applications, and Organizations," *Journal of Strategic Studies*, Vol. 37, No. 2, 2014, pp. 198–221.

Libicki, Martin, "Cyberspace Is Not a Warfighting Domain," *I/S: A Journal of Law and Policy for the Information Society*, Vol. 8. No. 2, 2012, pp. 321–336.

Losey, Stephen, "Goldfein's Gambit: Former Air Force Chief Weighs in on His Ambitious Plans," *Air Force Times*, September 18, 2016. As of May 24, 2018: https://www.airforcetimes.com/2016/09/18/goldfein-s-gambit-former-air-force-chiefs-weigh-in-on-his-ambitious-plans/

Losey, Stephen, "Information Operations Officers Get Their Own School," *Air Force Times*, March 13, 2018. As of July 2, 2018: https://www.airforcetimes.com/news/your-air- force/2018/03/13/information-operations-airmen-get-their-own-school/

Luiijf, Eric, Kim Besseling, and Patrick de Graaf, "Nineteen National Cyber Security Strategies," *International Journal of Critical Infrastructures*, Vol. 9, No. 1/2, 2013, pp. 3–31.

Lynn, William J., III, "A Military Strategy for the New Space Environment," *Washington Quarterly*, Vol. 34, No. 3, 2011, pp. 7–16.

Lynn, William J., "Defending a New Domain: The Pentagon's Cyberstrategy," *Council on Foreign Relations*, Vol. 89, 2010, pp. 97–108.

Marble, Julie L., W. F. Lawless, Ranjeev Mittu, Joseph Coyne, Myriam Abramson, and Ciara Sibley, "The Human Factor in Cybersecurity: Robust and Intelligent Defense," in Sushil Jajodia, Paulo Shakarian, V. S. Subrahmanian, Vipin Swarup, and Cliff Wang, eds., *Cyber Warfare*, New York: Springer, 2015.

Marine Corps Administration, *Implementation of the Regional, Culture and Language Familiarization Program*, Quantico, Va.: Marine Corps University, October 12, 2012.

Marine Corps Intelligence Activity, "Iraq Culture Smart Card," Quantico, Va., 2010.

Marine Corps Operating Concept, *How an Expeditionary Force Operates in the 21st Century,* September 2016. As of November 3, 2019:
https://www.mcwl.marines.mil/Portals/34/Images/MarineCorpsOperatingConceptSept 2016.pdf

Maurice, *Strategikon: Handbook of Byzantine Military Strategy*, trans. George T. Dennis, Philadelphia, Pa.: University of Pennsylvania Press, 1984.

Maybury, Mark T., "Science and Technology for the Human Domain," briefing, February 8, 2011.

McFate, Montgomery, and Janice H. Laurence, eds., *Social Science Goes to War: The Human Terrain System in Iraq and Afghanistan*, New York: Oxford University Press, 2015.

McGuffin, Chris, and Paul Mitchell, "On Domains: Cyber and the Practice of Warfare," *International Journal*, Vol. 69, No. 3, 2014, pp. 394–412.

MCIA—*See* Marine Corps Intelligence Activity.

McLeod, Gary, George Nacouzi, Paul Dreyer, Mel Eisman, Myron Hura, Krista S. Langeland, David Manheim, and Geoffrey Torrington, *Enhancing Space Resilience Through Non-Materiel Means*, Santa Monica, Calif.: RAND Corporation, RR-1067-AF, 2016. As of October 23, 2019:
https://www.rand.org/pubs/research_reports/RR1067.html

MCO—*See* United States Marine Corps, Marine Corps Order.

McNerney, Michael J., Ben Connable, S. Rebecca Zimmerman, Natasha Lander, Marek N. Posard, Jasen J. Castillo, Dan Madden, Ilana Blum, Aaron Frank, Benjamin J. Fernandes, In Hyo Seol, Christopher Paul, and Andrew Parasiliti, *National Will to Fight: Why Some States Keep Fighting and Others Don't,* Santa Monica, Calif.: RAND Corporation, RR-2477-A, 2018.

Ministry of Defence, UK Armed Forces, *Monthly Service Personnel Statistics,* October 1, 2017. As of June 13, 2018:
https://assets.publishing.service.gov.uk/government/uploads/system/uploads/attachment_data /file/659404/20171001_-_SPS.pdf

Navy Modeling and Simulation Office, homepage, website, undated. As of June 20, 2018:
https://www.mccdc.marines.mil/Units/OAD/MCMSO/NMSO/

Odierno, Raymond T., James F. Amos, William H. McRaven, *Strategic Landpower: Winning the Clash of Wills*, 2013. As of February 11, 2018:
https://api.army.mil/e2/c/downloads/310007.pdf

Pagano, Sabrina, and John A. Stevenson, *How Disagreement over Space Terms Can Create Barriers to Transparency in the Space Domain*, NSI Concept Paper, Arlington, Va.: Strategic Multi-layer Assessment (SMA), 2018. As of June 21, 2018:
http://nsiteam.com/sma- publications

Page, Ernest, "Modeling and Simulation, Experimentation, and Wargaming: Assessing a Common Landscape," *MITRE*, August 2016. As of June 18, 2018:
https://www.mitre.org/publications/technical-papers/modeling-and-simulation- experimentation -and-wargaming%E2%80%94assessing-a

Paul, Christopher, Jessica Yeats, Colin P. Clarke, Miriam Matthews, and Lauren Skrabala, *Assessing and Evaluating Department of Defense Efforts to Inform, Influence, and Persuade: Handbook for Practitioners*, Santa Monica, Calif.: RAND Corporation, RR-809/2-OSD, 2015. As of October 23, 2019:
https://www.rand.org/pubs/research_reports/RR809z2.html

Pawlyk, Oriana, "8 airmen needed for new human intelligence AFSC," *Air Force Times*, September 7, 2015. As of June 1, 2018:
https://www.airforcetimes.com/education- transition/jobs/2015/09/07/8-airmen-needed-for -new-human-intelligence-afsc/

Pollpeter, Kevin, "Space, the New Domain: Space Operation and Chinese Military Reforms," *Journal of Strategic Studies*, Vol. 39, 2016, pp. 709–727.

Price, David, "Lessons from Second World War Anthropology," *Anthropology Today*, Vol. 18, No. 3, 2002, pp. 14–20.

"Psychological Intelligence Analyst," job listing for British Psychological Society, 2016. As of June 13, 2018:
https://www.jobsinpsychology.co.uk/jobs/psychological-intelligence-analyst

Redden, Elizabeth, "Towards a 'Cross-Culturally Competent' Air Force," *Inside Higher Ed*, January 9, 2009.

Robinson, Jana, "Transparency and Confidence-Building Measures for Space Security," *Space Policy*, Vol. 37, No. 3, 2016, pp. 134–144.

Rollins, Amy, "Information Technology Complex Unveiled," webpage of Wright-Patterson Air Force Base, October 12, 2012. As of July 26, 2018:
http://www.wpafb.af.mil/News/Article-Display/Article/399516/information- technology -complex-unveiled/

Salerno, John J., Brian Romano, and Warren Geiler, "The National Operational Environment Model (NOEM)," *SPIE Proceedings*, Vol. 8060, May 21, 2011.

Samaan, Jean-Loup, "Cyber Command: The Rift in US Military Cyber-Strategy," *RUSI Journal*, Vol. 155, 2010, pp. 16–21.

Sandal, Gro Mjeldheim, and Dietrich Manzey, "Cross-Cultural Issues in Space Operations: A Survey Study Among Ground Personnel of the European Space Agency," *Acta Astronautica*, Vol. 65, 2009.

Sands, Robert R. Greene, "Thinking Differently: Unlocking the Human Domain in Support of the 21st Century Intelligence Mission," *Small Wars Journal*, 2013.

Sandy, David, J. Palmer, and J.-P. H. Hughes, *Maritime Information Warfare Concept of Operations (CONOPS)*, Royal Navy, Maritime Warfare Center, Green Paper 08-213, August 1, 2013. As of June 11, 2018:
http://c69011.r11.cf3.rackcdn.com/5c4b81ceb53b4c0bb224795cf0350c39-0x0.pdf

Schlenker, Barry R., "Social Psychology and Science," *Journal of Personality and Social Psychology*, Vol. 29, No. 1, 1974, pp. 1–15.

Schnell, Stephen, *Trust as a Currency: The Role of Relationships in the Human Domain*, Fort Leavenworth, Kan.: Army Command and General Staff College, January 2014.

Secretary of the Air Force Public Affairs, "Air Force Provides Approach for Security Cooperation," United States Air Force, January 19, 2017. As of May 22, 2018:
http://www.af.mil/News/Article-Display/Article/1054055/air-force-provides-approach-for-security-cooperation/

Security Forces Assistance Brigade, *Operating and Organizational Concept*, 2018. As of July 28, 2018:
https://fortbenningusa.org/wp-content/uploads/2018/04/TCM_SFAB_2018.pdf

SFAB—*See* Security Forces Assistance Brigade.

Snow, Shawn, "Marine Corps Strengthens Psychological Operations with New Job Field," *Marine Corps Times*, May 15, 2018a. As of June 16, 2018:
https://www.marinecorpstimes.com/news/your-marine-corps/2018/05/15/marines-corps-strengthen-psychological-operations-with-new-job-field/

Snow, Shawn, "Marines Look to Beef Psychological Ops with a Radio Station in a Box," *Marine Corps Times*, March 15, 2018b. As of June 15, 2018:
https://www.marinecorpstimes.com/news/your-marine-corps/2018/03/15/marines-look-to-beef-psychological-ops-with-a-radio-station-in-a-box/

Songip, A. R., Z. Md Zaki, K. Justoff, J. Prebagaran, and Ng. Boon-Beng, "Cyberspace: The Warfare Domain," *World Applied Sciences Journal*, Vol. 21, No. 1, 2013, pp. 1–7.

Spirtas, Michael, "Toward One Understanding of Multiple Domains," *C4ISRNet*, May 1, 2018. As of July 17, 2019:
https://www.c4isrnet.com/opinion/2018/05/01/toward-one-understanding-of-multiple-domains/

Suedfeld, Peter, "Historical Space Psychology: Early Terrestrial Explorations as Mars Analogues," *Planetary and Space Science*, Vol. 58, 2010, pp. 639–645.

Suedfeld, Peter, Jelena Brcic, and Katya Legkaia, "Coping with the Problems of Space Flight: Reports from Astronauts and Cosmonauts," *Acta Astronautica*, Vol. 65, 2009, pp. 312–324.

Suedfeld, Peter, Kasia E. Wilk, and Lindi Cassel, "Flying with Strangers: Postmission Reflections of Multinational Space Crews," in Douglas A. Vakoch, ed., *Psychology of Space Exploration: Contemporary Research in Historical Perspective*, Washington, D.C.: National Aeronautics and Space Administration, 2011.

Sun Tzu, *The Art of War*, trans. Ralph D. Sawyer, Boulder, Colo.: Westview Press, 1994.

Tafforin, C., "From Human Behavior to Human Factor in Aerospace, Astronautics and Space Operations," *SF Journal of Aviation and Aeronautical Science,* Vol. 1, No. 1, 2018, p.1003.

Training and Doctrine Command, Pam 525-3-0, *U.S. Army Capstone Concept*, December 19, 2012. As of November 2, 2019:
https://fas.org/irp/doddir/army/pam525-3-0.pdf

Training and Doctrine Command, Pam 525-3-6, *U.S. Army Functional Concept for Movement and Maneuver, 2020–2040*, Fort Eustis, Va., February 2017. As of November 2, 2019:
https://adminpubs.tradoc.army.mil/pamphlets/TP525-3-6.pdf

Training and Doctrine Command, Pam 525-8-5, *U.S. Army Functional Concept for Engagement*, Fort Eustis, Va., February 24, 2014. As of November 2, 2019:
https://adminpubs.tradoc.army.mil/pamphlets/TP525-8-2.pdf

TRADOC—*See* Training and Doctrine Command.

Travis, Donald, *Strategic Wargame 15-03: China Futures*, United States Army War College, Center for Strategic Leadership and Development, May 1, 2015. As of June 20, 2018:
http://www.csl.army.mil/LCDW/StrategicWargamingDivision/publications/China%20Future%20report%20AWC%2015%20May%2015.pdf

Understanding and Decision-Making, Joint Doctrine Publication 04, 2nd ed., Swindon, UK: Development, Concepts and Doctrine Centre, 2016. As of June 13, 2018:
https://assets.publishing.service.gov.uk/government/uploads/system/uploads/attachment_data/file/584177/doctrine_uk_understanding_jdp_04.pdf.

United States Air Force, *Air Force Culture, Region and Language Flight Plan*, Washington, D.C.: Headquarters, U.S. Air Force, 2009.

United States Air Force, "Officer Training School," webpage, 2017. As of December 12, 2017:
https://www.airforce.com/education/military-training/ots

United States Air Force Academy, "Outcomes," webpage, 2017. As of December 13, 2017:
https://www.usafa.edu/academics/outcomes/

United States Army Special Operations Command, *USASOC Strategy 2035*, April 2016. As of July 28, 2018:
http://www.soc.mil/Assorted%20Pages/USASOC2035%20Overview.pdf

United States Marine Corps, *Language, Regional Expertise and Culture (LREC) Strategy: 2016–2020*, Service Campaign Plan, 2016. As of November 3, 2019:
https://www.usmcu.edu/Portals/218/CAOCL/files/2016-20_USMC_LREC_Strategy_MCCDC_22Dec15.pdf?ver=2018-10-01-124416-513

United States Marine Corps, *Marine Corps Operating Concept for Information Operations,* February 4, 2013. As of November 3, 2019:
https://www.quantico.marines.mil/Portals/147/Docs/MCIOC/IORecruiting/MarineCorpsOperatingConceptforIO.pdf

United States Marine Corps, *Marine Corps Operating Concepts for a Changing Security Environment*, March 2006. As of June 2, 2020:
https://www.hsdl.org/?view&did=474274

United States Marine Corps, *Marine Corps Operations,* Marine Corps Doctrinal Publication 1-0 (w/ change 1), July 26, 2017. As of November 3, 2019:
https://www.marines.mil/Portals/1/Publications/MCDP%201-0%20W%20CH%201.pdf

United States Marine Corps, Marine Corps Order 3110.5, *Military Information Support Operations (MISO),* November 20, 2015. As of February 25, 2020:
https://www.marines.mil/Portals/1/MCO%203110.5.pdf

United States Marine Corps, *Warfighting*, MCDP 1, June 20, 1997. Accessed on February 27, 2020:
https://www.marines.mil/Portals/1/Publications/MCDP%201%20Warfighting.pdf

United States Special Operations Command, *Operating in the Human Domain*, August 3, 2015.

United States Special Operations Command, *Special Operations Forces Operating Concept,* A Whitepaper to Guide Future Special Operations Force Development, Directorate of Force Management and Development, Concept Development and Integration Office, Version 1.0, February 1, 2016. As of April 9, 2018:
https://www.jcs.mil/Portals/36/Documents/Doctrine/pubs/jp3_22.pdf?ver=2018-10-10-112450-103

USAFA—*See* United States Air Force Academy.

USASOC—*See* United States Army Special Operations Command.

USMC: LREC—*See* United States Marine Corps, Language, Regional Expertise and Culture Strategy.

USSOCOM—*See* United States Special Operations Command.

Vaishnav, Chintan, Nazli Choucri, and David Clark, "Cyber International Relations as an Integrated System," *Environmental Systems Decisions*, Vol. 33, 2013, pp. 561–576.

Valeriano, Brandon, and Ryan C. Maness, "The Dynamics of Cyber Conflict Between Rival Antagonists," *Journal of Peace Research*, Vol. 51, No. 3, 2014, pp. 347–360.

Varga, Margaret, Carsten Winkelholz, and Susan Traber-Burdin, "Cyber Situation Awareness," NATO/OTAN (STO-MP-IST-148), 2016. As of June 18, 2018: https://pdfs.semanticscholar.org/c182/7fb330e451d500605f98b868cd9c2dca7ada.pdf

Vautrinot, Suzanne M., "Sharing the Cyber Journey," *Strategic Studies Quarterly*, 2012, pp. 71– 87.

Vieane, Alex, Gregory Funke, Robert Gutzwiller, Vincent Mancuso, Ben Sawyer, and Christopher Wickens, "Addressing Human Factors Gaps in Cyber Defense," *Proceedings of the Human Factors and Ergonomics Society 2016 Annual Meeting*, 2016.

von Clausewitz, Carl, *On War*, ed. and trans. Michael Howard and Peter Paret, Princeton, N.J.: Princeton University Press, 1976.

Watts-Perotti, Jennifer, and David D. Woods, "How Anomaly Response Is Distributed Across Functionally Distinct Teams in Space Shuttle Mission Control," *Journal of Cognitive Engineering and Decision Making*, Vol. 1, No. 4, 2007, pp. 405–433.

Welch, Larry D., *Cyberspace: The Fifth Operational Domain*, Alexandria, Va.: IDA, 2011.

Westervelt, Eric, "How Russia Weaponized Social Media with 'Social Bots,'" NPR, November 5, 2017. As of July 2, 2018: https://www.npr.org/2017/11/05/562058208/how-russia- weaponized-social-media-with -social-bots

White House, *National Space Policy of the United States of America*, June 28, 2010. As of June 20, 2018: https://obamawhitehouse.archives.gov/sites/default/files/national_space_policy_6- 28-10.pdf

Woods, David D., and Emily S. Patterson, "How Unexpected Events Produce an Escalation of Cognitive and Coordinative Demands," in P. A. Hancock and P. Desmond, eds., *Stress Workload and Fatigue*, Hillsdale, N.J.: Lawrence Erlbaum, 2000.

Work, Bob, U.S. Deputy Secretary of Defense, "Wargaming and Innovation," memorandum for service principals, Washington, D.C., February 9, 2015.